S0-AZL-704

my TRUE TYPE

Clarifying Your Personality
Type, Preferences & Functions

Dr. A.J. Drenth

Copyright © 2014

A.J. Drenth

Published by Inquire Books

Edited by Brent Meredith

ISBN 978-0-9792168-4-8

All rights reserved. No part of this book may be reproduced in any form, electronic or mechanical, except for brief quotations, without written permission from the author. Myers-Briggs Type Indicator®, Myers-Briggs®, and MBTI® are trademarks or registered trademarks of the Myers-Briggs Type Indicator Trust in the United States and other countries.

CONTENTS

Part IV. Additional Clarification

INTRODUCTION

Who am I? What is my purpose? What should I be doing with my life? These are important questions that we all must wrestle with. Further complicating matters is the fact that we live in a world where firm answers are increasingly hard to come by. While the options available to us continue to expand exponentially, there seem to be fewer reliable standards for guiding and informing our decisions. This can leave us feeling lost and overwhelmed, unsure of where to turn for answers to our most pressing questions.

It is out of this state of dizziness and confusion that we often come to personality typing, or what is sometimes called *typology*. We come seeking insight into who we are and what we should do with our lives. We crave a clearer sense of purpose and direction.

More specifically, we come to typology seeking a more objective understanding of who we are. We want to know where we fit into the bigger picture of humanity. Through the objective lens of typology, we hope to gain greater confidence and certainty about who we are, as well as the roles we might play in the collective drama.

Given these high hopes and expectations, it is unfortunate that so many people encounter an unexpected hurdle at the very outset of their typological journey—type confusion. Although they may have been furnished a type (e.g., INFJ) after taking a personality assessment, upon further investigation, they may come to doubt its accuracy. This may prompt them to retake the test, sample other tests, or read more about the types to ascertain greater clarity. Even if interesting at first, this can become a rather frustrating affair, as what began with an expectation of objective answers starts to feel more like a wild goose chase. This may even lead some folks to throw in the towel, concluding that typology is not for them or is not worth the requisite time and effort. Others may turn to alternate personality systems, hoping to find an easier or better fit.

I am no exception. The above scenario is as much my story as anyone else's. I spent several years trying to understand myself through a variety of personality frameworks. I studied Jung, Myers-Briggs, Keirsey, Eysenck, the Enneagram, the Big Five, physiognomy, and more. While I found some degree of truth and resonance in all these approaches, it wasn't until I began working with my colleague, Elaine Schallock, that I came to see the Jungian / Myers-Briggs model as my clear favorite. Schallock's insights into type theory, the functions, the "functional stack," and the inferior function took Jung's work to a new level of depth, clarity, and applicability. Through years of discussions (and debates) with Schallock, my perspective gradually shifted from one of typological relativism to one of deep respect and appreciation for the Jungian framework. I also came to see and understand my type (INTP) more vividly than ever, making it hard to imagine how I could have typed myself otherwise.

Having been transformed from a skeptic to an interpreter and advocate of Jungian typology, I have much that I want to share and explore. But before beginning our foray into the nitty-gritty of type, I would like to briefly make the case for why typology is important and why it is worth your time and effort.

Why It's Important to Know Your Type

For starters, knowing your type is important because "being yourself" or "being true to yourself" seems to require that you first "know yourself." This seems especially true for introverts, many of whom feel it necessary to understand themselves and clarify their identity before they can authentically engage with the world.

But why is it important to be ourselves? One reason is that being ourselves is more satisfying and rewarding than trying to be someone we are not. When we understand and align with our natural strengths, we are more apt to experience what Mihaly Csikszentmihalyi has described as "flow." Flow is a pleasurable and satisfying state, involving a deep sense of immersion and absorption in what we are doing. It occurs when our minds have just the right amount of challenge and stimulation, and when are well suited to the activity. In other words, flow results when *what we do aligns with who we are.*

Because flow experiences are deeply rewarding, we naturally seek them out. We work to identify careers and relationships that provide us with consistent opportunities for achieving flow. But as we discussed earlier, modern life, with its dizzying number of options and possibilities, can leave us feeling ambivalent or paralyzed by indecision. While we may have an implicit sense of who we are and what we are good at, it can still be overwhelming to make big decisions regarding our careers, relationships, and so on. It is here where typology can step in and provide helpful guidance and insight.

By identifying our type, we can know what type of person we are and from which mold we were cast. Like the acorn destined to become an oak, each personality type is designed to follow a given path, even if wide enough to allow for individual variations along the way. By understanding our type, as well as its prospective course of growth and development, we become more consciously aware of what it means to "be" and "become" our true, authentic selves.

Knowing and understanding our type also carries certain moral implications. One could certainly argue, as Socrates famously did, that self-knowledge is foundational to the well-lived, virtuous life. One might also suggest that a lack of self-knowledge, or what we might call *self-ignorance*, is equally, if not more dangerous than other forms of ignorance. Fortunately, typology can illuminate aspects of ourselves we might otherwise be blind to. It can reveal deep psychological patterns and structures that furtively influence our thoughts, attitudes, and behaviors. And with this awareness comes the freedom to shake loose from the trappings and shackles of less optimal patterns.

Not only can knowing our type contribute to our psychological health and growth as individuals, but it can also enhance our collective health and well-being. Just as the parts of a healthy body work together in a unified way, a healthy society requires that all personality types function optimally and utilize their natural strengths. Equally important, typology helps us understand why others may think and behave differently than we do. By understanding why others think and behave as they do, we can more readily appreciate them for who they are, thereby diminishing the urge to criticize or change them into something they are not.

What is a Personality Type?

I love illustrating typological concepts with analogies. Analogies allow us to use familiar or commonplace ideas to understand more obscure or less familiar ones. I would therefore like to begin this section by suggesting that personality types are a lot like trees.

Most people aren't so brave as to deny the existence of different types of trees. An oak tree, for instance, clearly displays characteristics that distinguish it from other types of trees. Likewise, it is hard to deny the reality of different personality types. Just as oaks are inherently different from cherries, so it is with ENFJs, INFPs, ISTPs, etc.

Taking our analogy one step further, just as oak trees do not change into cherry trees, I will argue that our essential personality type is unlikely to change over time. Since our type and its features (preferences, functions, etc.) are part of the core framework of our personality, they are too deep and too fundamental to undergo significant modification. In this respect, a personality type is similar to the foundation of a house. While a house may undergo any number of revisions and improvements, its foundation and basic structure are typically left unaffected.

With that said, there are less foundational aspects of our personality that can and do change over time. If this were not the case, personal growth would not be possible. Just as we make improvements and modifications to our homes, our personality grows and develops across the lifespan. I discuss the process and phases of type development in my recent book, *The 16 Personality Types*.

It is also important to recognize the collective aspect of type. After all, the very notion of types could have never arisen if we looked only at ourselves. Nor could it have emerged if we viewed each individual as entirely unique. To the contrary, the notion of types developed from the recognition that people display patterns of thought, attitude, and behavior that are similar to those of some people, while differing from those of others. Hence, typology is at once an individual and collective enterprise.

Finally, I would like to mention a parallel between typology and physics. Namely, the psychological laws and patterns of human behavior are in many ways comparable to the physical laws of the universe. The basic premise of typology is that human behavior, like the physical universe, is fashioned according to recurring structures and predictable laws that can be rationally discerned and described. This links up with what we discussed earlier about the objective nature of typology. So just as physicists study the physical universe objectively, typologists work to objectively map the human psyche.

A Brief History of Type

In his 1913 classic, *Psychological Types*, Carl Jung propounded the basic theoretical framework for what is now the most popular personality system in the world. Most remarkably, Jung did not rely on formal research methods in developing his theory of the types. Nor did he develop or utilize formal assessments for the sake of type identification. Instead, Jung relied largely on his own powers of observation and insight in both developing his theories and identifying individuals of various types.

Although Jung spoke generally of introverts and extraverts, he eventually delineated eight psychological functions (Ni, Ne, Si, Se, Ti, Te, Fi, Fe) as a more accurate means of understanding the types. More specifically, he focused on identifying an individual's dominant function, as well as, to a lesser extent, the auxiliary function.

Because Jung never developed a standardized personality assessment tool, his ideas were slow to catch on among the general public. It was not until Isabel Myers and her mother, Katherine Briggs, entered the scene that Jung's theory began its ascendance toward widespread recognition. Myers and Briggs developed the *Myers-Briggs Type Indicator*®, or what is commonly known as the MBTI®, as a way of applying and popularizing Jung's ideas.

While Jung spoke mostly in terms of a type's preferred *functions* (e.g. Ni, Se), Myers and Briggs introduced and emphasized the notion of *preferences* (i.e., E, I, S, N, T, F, J, P). Although still rooted in Jung's theory, Myers and Briggs likely saw the preferences as more amenable to objective assessment than Jung's multi-dimensional functions. Despite the different emphases of a preference versus function-based approach, these two approaches can and arguably should be used in tandem.

In many respects, Myers and Briggs were correct in seeing the preference-based approach as more user-friendly, since it is more easily comprehended and requires less background knowledge. However, individuals seeking a deeper understanding of themselves and their personality type must eventually dive into the functions. This book will incorporate both approaches, exploring the typing process from the perspective of the Myers-Briggs preferences as well as the Jungian functions.

More recent advances in type theory have highlighted the importance of understanding the less conscious functions, particularly the *inferior function*, which we will soon discuss. This can be seen in Marie-Louise Von Franz's exploration of the inferior function in *Jung's Typology* (1971), as well as in Naomi Quenk's 1993 book, *Beside Ourselves*, later renamed, *Was That Really Me?*

For the last decade or so, Elaine Schallock and I have continued to refine and advance type theory, including intensive explorations of the preferences, functions, inferior function, function pairs, and functional stack. All of these elements will be enumerated in this book, providing you with the most up-to-date information for accurately identifying and understanding your personality type.

The Preferences

According to Myers and Briggs, each personality type has four basic preferences, with each type preferring either introversion (I) or extraversion (E), sensing (S) or intuition (N), thinking (T) or feeling (F), and judging (J) or perceiving (P).

For example, INFJs prefer I, N, F, and J more than E, S, T, and P. This does not mean that INFJs never utilize E, S, T, or P, but when given the chance, they prefer to use I, N, F, or J.

To illustrate what a personality preference is, I like to compare it hand dominance. As we all know, a right-handed person will prefer to use her right hand for the majority of tasks, especially those requiring fine motor skills, such as writing. This of course doesn't mean that she never uses her left hand, but only that it tends to play more of a supportive, rather than a dominant or leading, role.

The same is true for our personality preferences. While we may at times use our non-dominant preferences, in most situations we prefer to lead with our dominant ones. Not only does this feel more comfortable and natural, but typically produces better results. We will explore each of the eight preferences in greater detail in upcoming chapters.

The Functions

Of the eight preferences, four of them—sensing, intuition, thinking, and feeling—also double as functions. Extraversion and introversion do not qualify as functions because, according to Jung, they primarily represent our preferred *direction of energy and attention*. Extraverts direct their energy and attention *outwardly*, toward people, objects, events, possibilities, etc. Introverts, by contrast, direct their focus *inwardly*, toward themselves—their own thoughts, feelings, intuitions, sensations, etc.

Not only did Jung believe that individuals were characteristically introverted or extraverted, but also that each function assumes an introverted or extraverted direction. Thus, when S, N, T, and F are directed inwardly (I) or outwardly (E), we end up with eight functions (Si, Se, Ni, Ne, Ti, Te, Fi, Fe).

But what about judging and perceiving? Why aren't they considered functions? The answer is they do play a role in the functions, only less explicitly. Namely, sensing and intuition are considered to be perceiving functions. They are in charge of absorbing, extracting, retaining, or synthesizing information. Thinking and feeling are judging functions. Their purpose is to evaluate information and make decisions that contribute to structure, order, and predictability. Hence, the eight functions can be subdivided into perceiving and judging functions as follows:

The Judging Functions:
- Introverted Thinking (Ti)
- Extraverted Thinking (Te)
- Introverted Feeling (Fi)
- Extraverted Feeling (Fe)

The Perceiving Functions:
- Introverted Sensing (Si)
- Extraverted Sensing (Se)
- Introverted Intuition (Ni)
- Extraverted Intuition (Ne)

We will examine each of these functions in greater detail in future chapters.

The Functional Stack

Each personality type uses four functions that comprise its functional stack. These functions are ordered according to their relative degree of strength and development, as well as their availability for conscious employment. The most developed and conscious function is called the "dominant function," which is followed by the auxiliary, tertiary, and inferior functions respectively.

The dominant function represents the core strength and defining characteristic of each type. When engrossed in an activity that fully engages the dominant function, we tend to feel alert and alive, doing what we were "born to do." The auxiliary function, which can also be useful and readily developed, might be viewed as the co-pilot or sidekick to the dominant. Falling toward the bottom of the functional stack, the tertiary and inferior are less conscious and developed than the top two functions. However diminutive their conscious presence, the less conscious functions play an important role in each type's personality dynamics.

Dominant Function: "The Captain"; the signature tool and strength of the personality type

Auxiliary Function: "The Sidekick"; chief assistant to the dominant function

Tertiary Function: "The Adolescent"; relatively unconscious and undeveloped

Inferior Function: "The Child"; the least conscious and developed of the four functions

Here is the INTP's functional stack, which we'll use as an example:

Dominant Function: Introverted Thinking (Ti)

Auxiliary Function: Extraverted Intuition (Ne)

Tertiary Function: Introverted Sensing (Si)

Inferior Function: Extraverted Feeling (Fe)

In considering the INTP's functional stack, you may have noticed something curious. Namely, INTPs (and all other types for that matter) use a thinking, feeling, sensing, and intuiting function. This may be a bit confusing at first, since there is no indication of sensing (S) or feeling (F) in their I, N, T, or P preferences. If you look carefully, however, you will notice that their S and F functions are situated below their T and N functions. This tells us that INTPs prefer to use T and N (or more specifically Ti and Ne) more than S (i.e., Si) or F (i.e., Fe). See Appendix II to view the functional stacks of all the personality types.

J-P Criteria

Observant readers may have noticed another curious fact about INTPs' functional stack, namely, that despite their status as a P type, their dominant function (Ti) is actually a *judging* function. The other IP types (i.e., ISTP, INFP, ISFP) also employ a dominant judging function (Ti or Fi). The situation is reversed for IJs (i.e., INTJ, ISTJ, INFJ, ISFJ), who use a dominant perceiving function (Ni or Si). This of course makes things more complicated when it comes to understanding IPs and IJs as judgers versus perceivers. Although we will reserve further discussion of this issue until Chapter 6 and Chapter 16, at this point, you should work to familiarize yourself with the following J-P criteria:

1. A given type's J-P designation (i.e., the fourth letter of the type) refers largely to its outer (i.e., extraverted) presentation. Hence, J types will extravert a judging attitude (firm, decisive, opinionated, etc.), while P types will display a perceiving attitude (open, flexible, receptive, etc.).

2. For extraverts, the nature of the dominant function (i.e., its status as a judging or perceiving function) matches their J-P designation. For example, ENTPs' dominant function, Ne, is a perceiving function and ENTJs' dominant function, Te, is a judging function.

3. For introverts, things are more confusing, since the nature of their dominant function opposes their J-P designation. We saw this with INTPs above. Namely, despite being classified as a P type, INTPs' dominant function (Ti) is a judging function. To understand why INTPs and other IPs are considered P rather than J types, see "rule" number one above.

4. In light of the above, we can make the following associations between the functions and preferences of the various types:

- Si = SJ types (i.e., Si used as the dominant or auxiliary)
- Se = SP types
- Ni = NJ types
- Ne = NP types
- Ti = TP types
- Te = TJ types
- Fi = FP types
- Fe = FJ types

Purpose & Overview

The chief purpose of this book is to equip you with the knowledge necessary to clarify and better understand your personality type. In conjunction with the information presented in *The 16 Personality Types*, it strives to deepen your understanding of the essential features of your personality type, including your preferences, functions, and functional stack.

To combat the inherent challenges of personality typing, Part I lays some preliminary groundwork for the typing process.

Chapter 1 explores some of the common barriers and roadblocks to effective typing, including the confounding effects of "nurture," personality development, and the inferior function. It also touches on the shortcomings of personality tests with respect to accurate type diagnosis.

In Chapter 2, we consider numerous tips strategies, both general and specific, for effective personality typing. These strategies will prove useful as you move through the remainder of the book, helping you further refine and clarify your typological understanding.

Part II (Chapters 3-6) takes a careful look at the nature and typing criteria for each of the eight preferences: introversion (I), extraversion (E), sensing (S), intuition (N), thinking (T), feeling (F), judging (J), and perceiving (P). Toward the end of each chapter, we will explore some common typing pitfalls, or "mistypings," such as why an introvert might misclassify as an extravert, or vice-versa.

Building on Part II, Part III (Chapters 7-15) entails an in-depth survey of the eight functions: Introverted Intuition (Ni), Extraverted Intuition (Ne), Introverted Sensing (Si), Extraverted Sensing (Se), Introverted Thinking (Ti), Extraverted Thinking (Te), Introverted Feeling (Fi), and Extraverted Feeling (Fe). In addition to carefully describing the nature and presentation of each of the functions, we will explore recent neuroscientific research detailing their association with specific brain regions and states of neurological activity.

In Part IV (Chapter 16), we dive even deeper into the types, examining how the structuring of the functional stack reveals important and commonly overlooked similarities between EJs and IPs, as well as EPs and IJs. While adding a layer of theoretical complexity and nuance, it should nonetheless prove useful for further clarifying and understanding your type. This chapter also summarizes some of the essential characteristics of EPs, EJs, IPs, and IJs, including touching on issues related to their respective inferior functions.

Part I

EFFECTIVE TYPING:
BARRIERS & STRATEGIES

Chapter 1

BARRIERS TO
EFFECTIVE TYPING

Since identifying our true type is rarely as simple or straightforward as it seems, it is important to consider potential barriers or roadblocks to accurate typing. This will comprise our aim in this chapter. Specifically, we will consider the confounding role of nurture, personality development, and the inferior function in type identification. We will also touch on some potential shortcomings of personality tests with regard to accurate type diagnosis.

The Confounding Role of Nurture

One of the major barriers to accurate typing involves the confounding effects of "nurture." By nurture, I am referring to the cumulative effects of past and present circumstances—culture, family, childhood, etc.—on our personality.

Generally speaking, typology tells us much about the "nature" side of our personality, or what we might think of as our psychological DNA. It tells us very little, however, about the effects of nurture. So if we are willing to grant nature and nurture their respective contributions to the big picture of personality, which I think is entirely reasonable, we must conclude that typology is limited in its capacity to predict or explain the totality of our personality.

Although nurture does not change our basic personality type, it can in some ways cloud or impair our ability to accurately perceive our true type. Imagine, for instance, an extravert raised as an only child in a rural area, with no one but her parents to talk to. Such a child would seem far more likely to develop her introverted capacities than one raised with multiple siblings, which may in turn compromise her ability to grasp her true status as an extravert.

Jobs and careers may also leave their mark on our personality, as well as our perceptions of it. For example, working a highly structured job with predefined hours might cause perceiving types to resemble or see themselves as judgers. Similarly, unstructured work might lead judgers to fancy themselves perceivers.

In light of these examples, accurate typing requires that we effectively distinguish between nature (i.e., our true type) and nurture (i.e., the conditioned features overlaying and interlacing with our type). At minimum, this involves being able to distance ourselves from our present circumstances in order to better grasp the larger, historical picture of our type.

Personality Development

Our level of personal growth, or what is sometimes called "type development," can also impact our ability to clearly recognize our type. In *The 16 Personality Types*, I discuss the three phases of type development for each of the personality types. Of these phases, Phase II is the most likely to derail our attempts at type diagnosis.

Phase II begins in late childhood and, for some people, may continue for decades. As the pressures and responsibilities involved with transitioning to adulthood grow more pronounced, we often experience a commensurate spike in identity confusion, and with it, type confusion. Further complicating matters, Phase II also entails a struggle for ascendancy between the dominant and inferior function. In short, because so much is happening in Phase II, both internally and externally, identity confusion and type confusion are commonplace.

The Inferior Function

In the previous chapter, we learned that the dominant function represents a type's signature strength. While the dominant is the most conscious and well-developed of the functions, the mostly unconscious inferior function is in many respects its "other half." Put together, they comprise a functional whole. And because the psyche desperately wants to be whole, all types are inclined to pursue, and to some degree identify with, their inferior function.

The reputed "opposite" of the dominant function, the inferior represents a new and exciting mode of existence. It is commonly experienced and described as intensely pleasurable, even magical. For example, when a thinking type with inferior feeling experiences powerful feelings of love or infatuation, he may feel he's been transported to a whole new world. Dominant feelers may experience something similar in moments of logical clarity.

Because of the power and allure of the inferior function, it contributes to no small amount of identity and type confusion. Indeed, for many of us, it is only after exploring and experimenting with the inferior function that we come to clearly recognize (or remember) who we really are (i.e., to accurately identify our dominant function). In this sense, we are like children who must make mistakes to "learn our lessons." We must toy with, and even get burned by, the inferior before we remember and acknowledge our primary strength. And because most people have never even heard of the inferior function, it stands as one of the most insidious and overlooked sources of type confusion.

Shortcomings of Personality Assessments

Among the more common methods of type assessment is administering self-report questionnaires or "personality tests." One of the more alluring features of personality tests is they provide a quick and objective result. Simply check some boxes, tabulate the results, and "whoala!" we have a type! Unfortunately, the effects of nurture, circumstances, personality development, the inferior function, and other factors may combine to create confusion in test responses. Clearly, there is a glut of information test-takers must sort through as they go about formulating their responses.

Making matters worse, personality tests themselves are far from perfect. Test-takers often feel that certain test items are unclear, misleading or confusing. Test items may also fail to measure the personality traits that most effectively represent or relate to one's type. Some questions may assess traits that vary widely among individuals of the same personality type. We encounter a similar problem in many descriptions and profiles of the types. Namely, when essential information is omitted, or non-essential information included, type confusion is bound to arise.

Chapter 2

STRATEGIES FOR ACCURATE TYPING

In light of the previous chapter, it is clear that plenty can go wrong in the process of discerning our type. In recognition of this sobering reality, I wished to start this chapter by suggesting that there are no magic bullets for identifying your type. While we like to think that personality tests are, or could feasibly be, magic bullets, they are really just a piece of a larger typing process. Identifying and understanding your type is best done through a multi-pronged approach, involving *an ongoing process of learning, understanding, and insight.*

A key element of the typing process is understanding the personality framework—the preferences, functions, functional stack, and so on. Equally critical is accurately assessing and understanding yourself in light of that framework. As you explore and engage with the framework and its concepts, you will become aware of things you never noticed or understood about yourself. It is only by working to understand the framework, as well as your personality in light of the framework, that a deeper understanding of your type will emerge.

To facilitate this process, you will want to take a few personality tests, such as the *Type Clarifier* (Appendix I), the *MBTI*, or other tests on Personality Junkie. You will also want to explore some type descriptions, or what are commonly called "type profiles," such as those included in *The 16 Personality Types*. The problem with many type profiles is they provide rather generic descriptions of the types based on a cursory understanding of the preferences. And it can be difficult to confidently identify your personality type without also having a working knowledge of the functions.

Let's say, for instance, you are working to decide whether you are an INFJ or an INFP. While these two types may seem rather similar at first glance, sharing three of four preferences, they actually share NONE of the same functions. This contributes to substantial differences between these two types that may well be missed if thinking only in terms of the preferences.

Another typing strategy involves asking a perceptive friend, family member, counselor, or type practitioner to discuss your personality with you. They can offer you an outsider's perspective, which you can then compare and contrast with your own observations. Since extraverts are disposed to looking outward before looking inward, they may find input from others particularly helpful and reassuring.

The above strategies—understanding the personality framework, taking personality assessments, exploring type profiles, self-reflection, and discussing your personality with others—are the "bread and butter" methods of identifying your true type. For the remainder of this chapter, we will explore some additional strategies that can help you clarify your type.

Explore Childhood Patterns

Adulthood brings demands and pressures that may obscure our type's natural tendencies and preferences. Introverts, for instance, may view it practically necessary to routinely engage with others in the workplace, which over time, could feasibly lead them to lose sight of their true preference.

To prevent our self-appraisals from being skewed by current circumstances, it can be helpful to reflect on your childhood attitudes and behaviors, particularly those exhibited in times of leisure (e.g., summer break).

In reflecting on my childhood, for instance, I remember having an early love for words, language, and word patterns. Throughout my elementary school years, I took great pride in maintaining a running list of homophones (okay, so I've always been a bit nerdy!). I also enjoyed making puns (still do), writing limericks, and playing word games with my mother. Looking back, my interest in language, including its underlying structure and patterns, was an early clue to my status as an intuitive type.

As you study the preferences and functions in the upcoming chapters, I encourage you to consider how each may (or may not) have been evident in your childhood.

Which Type(s) are You Least Like?

While it is normal to focus the lion's share of your attention on the personality types that describe you best, it can also be useful to do the opposite—to consider which types resemble you the least.

As an exercise, consider making a list of three or four personality types that best describe your personality. From those, select the one that is least like you. If your selection happens to be an extraverted type, this may help confirm your status as an introvert, if a sensing type, it may confirm your status as an intuitive, and so on.

An INTP friend of mine, for example, was confident in his status as an NT type. However, he was unsure whether he was an INTP, ENTP, or INTJ. From this, it was clear that, of the four NT types, he was least like the ENTJ. This indirectly suggested that he was both an introvert and a perceiver, which ultimately helped him clarify his status as an INTP.

Which Function(s) Do You Use the Least?

A similar approach can be used with the functions, in which you work to identify your least used functions.

For example, the Extraverted Feeling (Fe) and Extraverted Thinking (Te) functions often present as bold, opinionated, and forceful, especially when used as a type's dominant function. So if you were to see these traits as largely uncharacteristic of your historical personality, Introverted Feeling (Fi) or Introverted Thinking (Ti) could well be your dominant function.

What is Your Enantiodromia?

The central psychological challenge for each personality type involves effectively resolving the ongoing tug-of-war between its dominant and inferior functions. Jung introduced the term *enantiodromia* to describe this struggle of psychic opposites.

For instance, both ESPs and INJs must navigate persistent tensions between Se and Ni, between broad external sensory perception (Se) and intensive inner intuition (Ni). With regard to typing, the idea here would be to think of each type's dominant and inferior functions as pairs, or what I like to call "function pairs." Hence, both ESPs' and INJs' chief psychological struggle will involve the Ni-Se (or, if you prefer, Se-Ni) function pair.

So let's say you're trying to decide whether you're an INFJ or an ENFJ. Since both of these types use the same four functions, only in a different order, you might ask yourself which function pair you wrestle with the most. For INFJs (and INTJs), the answer would likely be the Ni-Se function pair. For ENFJs (and ESFJs), it is apt to be the Fe-Ti function pair. We will explore each of the four function pairs (i.e., Te-Fi, Fe-Ti, Se-Ni, Ne-Si) in upcoming chapters.

Put Inconsistencies in Perspective

If you're like most people, you have probably encountered some incongruities between your own self-perceptions and the way your personality type is described. This can relate to a number of factors, including the relative ordering of the functions in the functional stack. For instance, if you are an ISFP and Extraverted Sensing (Se) is your auxiliary function, your Se may be tempered by your overall status as an introvert. Hence, you may fail to identify with the more pronounced Se characteristics displayed by ESPs. This does not mean you are not an ISFP or that you do not use Se, but only that your introversion may be limiting the extremity of your extraverted functions.

Furthermore, because reality does not always align with our perceptions of it, the typing process requires some willingness to accept that, despite ostensible exceptions or inconsistencies, general psychological laws and patterns are nevertheless at work. For certain individuals, especially P types, this can be a tall order. It can, after all, be difficult to accept something that deviates from our personal experiences or perceptions. But just as we don't personally experience the world as round, there are times when we must rely on more objective tools and methods (e.g., satellite images) to provide a more accurate and comprehensive picture of reality. So while you may at times find it difficult to see your type through a wall of apparent inconsistencies, this doesn't mean that types don't exist or that you won't eventually come to see your own type more clearly.

It is probably worth reiterating that typology looks at general patterns manifesting across the population. At the population level, individual differences fade and general similarities (and differences) come to the fore. Through the process of zooming out, variations and anomalies are lost or blurred, leaving us with general patterns and outlines. It is these general patterns—constituting the types, preferences, functions, etc.—that are most important and foundational to personality typology.

Avoid Over-Focusing on Particulars

Related to the act of zooming out is avoiding over-focusing on any specific trait or detail of your personality. For instance, it is dubious to assume that being talkative automatically qualifies you as an extravert. Due to the myriad complexities and confounding factors at play in personality, placing too much emphasis on any one trait can easily lead you astray.

The trick in determining your type is to take the totality of what you know about your personality and work to discern its underlying structure (i.e., type). I realize this is easier said than done, particularly for sensing types, who are naturally more attuned to specifics and details than underlying patterns. Truth be told, INJs are probably the types best suited for apprehending these sorts of deep patterns. Hence, consulting with an INJ, especially an INFJ, may prove helpful for synthesizing and making sense of the various elements of your personality, thereby clarifying your true type.

Part II

CLARIFYING YOUR PREFERENCES

As we saw in the Introduction, one approach to discerning your personality type is to identify your four preferences (i.e., E or I, S or N, T or F, J or P).

One question I frequently encounter with respect to the preferences is whether it is possible to sit on the fence between two preferences; that is, to have no real preference at all. If you've spent time perusing typology forums online, you may have noticed people inserting an "x" in place of one or two letters of their type (e.g., ExFP), suggesting they have adopted this line of thinking. Although this practice seems reasonable if one remains unclear as to his or her true type, the notion of not having a preference is dubious from the perspective of type theory.

The problem with the notorious "x" is that it not only implies a lack of clarity with respect to one's preferences, but also one's functions. For instance, typing oneself as an IxFJ not only denotes S-N ambivalence, but also uncertainty with regard to using the Si-Ne function pair versus the Ni-Se function pair. In my view, a lack of clarity in all these areas suggests either a deficit in self-knowledge or a lack of insight into the preferences and functions. If type is the deep psychological structure we believe it to be, the idea that an individual can routinely oscillate between function pairs, displaying no preference for one over the other, is dubious. This would be akin to being ambidextrous to the point of having no preference for writing with the left or right hand. While this could feasibly be the case for a few rare individuals, it is certainly not the norm.

Chapter 3

INTROVERSION (I) vs. EXTRAVERSION (E)

Broadly speaking, the notions of introversion and extraversion highlight the distinction between self (I) and world (E), individual (I) and collective (E). The ramifications of this E-I divide can be readily observed in everyday life, especially in politics. We often hear, for instance, of people rallying for individual rights, individual liberties, personal privacy, and so on. Words like "personal," "private," and "individual" key us into the fact that an introverted perspective is probably being discussed or defended. On the other side of the spectrum, we see people advocating for public or collective laws, systems, and values. These represent a more extraverted approach. In politics, as well as in everyday human affairs, we see a constant tension and see-sawing between the desires of the individual and those of the collective, between introverted and extraverted perspectives.

The E-I dimension also highlights a fundamental distinction between inner experience (I) and outer experience (E), subjective (I) and objective (E). Such differences might become apparent, for instance, when discussing your personality traits with a friend. Since you alone are privy to your first-person world of inner experience, you may see and describe your personality quite differently than your friend might. This would seem particularly likely if you are an introvert, since introverts often feel that others fail to know or understand them for who they really are (i.e., for their inner selves).

Over the last few decades or so, conceptions of introverts and extraverts have found their way out of esoteric obscurity and into everyday discourse. In the public mind, introverts are often conceived as shy, timid, reserved, and perhaps a bit geeky or socially awkward. Television shows like *The Big Bang Theory* hyperbolize notions of the nerdy, awkward introvert.

Extraverts, in contrast, are commonly conceived as more outgoing, aggressive, popular, and physically impressive. In pop culture, athletes and cheerleaders are often portrayed as extraverts, while the geeks and artsy kids are depicted as more introverted.

While certainly exaggerated for their entertainment value, there is at least a kernel of truth in these depictions; they are not mere fantasy. People watchers can surely attest to the existence of E-I differences, even if typically revealed in less dramatic ways.

Despite growing public awareness of E-I distinctions, many people struggle when it comes to identifying their own preference. They may fail to resonate with images of the awkward introvert or those of the gregarious extravert. For such persons (and you may be one of them), a more careful and detailed analysis is required.

Jung's Theory of Introversion & Extraversion

Jung had much to say about E-I differences. Indeed, before he developed his theory of the functions, he saw only two primary personality types—introverts and extraverts. In *Psychological Types*, he extensively explores E-I differences as manifest in art, poetry, and philosophy. While I certainly recommend the entirety of Jung's work to interested readers, what is most important for our present purpose is Jung's foundational premise that E and I represent *opposite directions of attention and energy flow.*

More specifically, Jung conceived introverts' energy and attention as *inwardly directed*—aimed at the self and its interests. Related to this inner focus, Jung associated introversion with *depth and intensity*. This can be seen, for instance, in the introvert's tendency to invest a great deal of time and energy into a single project, problem, person, or interest area.

Conversely, Jung saw extraverts' focus as *outwardly directed*, leading them to act more extensively. We see this in their tendency to distribute their time and energies across a broader range of people, interests, or activities.

Independent (I) vs. Collective-Minded (E)

Especially in the first half of life, *introverts are most interested in discovering exactly what it is they have to offer the world.* They see self-knowledge as a prerequisite to authentic action. Without an adequate map of themselves, they feel lost and aimless. For introverts, external circumstances are far less important than self-understanding and self-direction. Once they have a sense of who they are and what they should be doing, they feel they can be happy anywhere.

Extraverts, by contrast, are *most interested in discovering what the world has to offer them.* Instead of turning inward for direction, they look without. Instead of increasing their self-knowledge, they augment their "world-knowledge." While the self is the introvert's forum for exploration and direction, the world is center stage for extraverts.

In looking inward first, introverts can be viewed as more independent-minded than extraverts. In many respects, *introverts trust themselves more than they trust the world.* More specifically, ITPs place great trust in their own logic, strategies, and methods (Ti), IFPs in their personal tastes, feelings, and moral sentiments (Fi), ISJs in their personal routines and cherished traditions (Si), and INJs in their impressions and insights (Ni). Of all the introverted types, ISJs are probably the least independent-minded due to their reliance on historical or cultural traditions and authorities.

In being more outwardly oriented, the extraverted mind is more influenced by and dependent on the world. In some respect, *extraverts trust others, or more broadly, "the world," more than they trust themselves.* More specifically, ESPs trust appearances (Se), EFJs relationships and reputations (Fe), ENPs circulating theories and ideas (Ne), and ETJs collective standards and methods (Te). Of all the extraverted types, ENPs are probably the most independent-minded since, as dominant intuitives, they are more heavily influenced by their own subconscious mind.

In light of their independent-mindedness, introverts are more concerned with the notion of authenticity. For them, this means identifying and holding firm to their own preferences and convictions, even when others are doing things differently. They are wary of "selling out" or "selling their soul" for the sake of conformity or convention.

Extraverts, on the other hand, are more concerned with fitting in or keeping pace with what others are doing. For them, authenticity involves synchronizing with the outside world. If they can attune to and engage with what is happening "out there," they feel authentically satisfied. In many respects, extraverts are happiest when they "lose themselves" in external affairs. Especially early in life, they are generally content to let the world define or direct them (again, ENPs may be somewhat of an exception). Rather than searching inwardly for self-definition, they root their identity and decisions in external affairs, ideas, and affiliations.

Reflection (I) vs. Action (E)

Introverts in general, and IJs in particular, tend to reflect before they act. They approach life carefully and cautiously in order to avoid making mistakes. They take a "measure twice, cut once approach." This is true with respect to spending money, having children, assuming external commitments, and so on. Although IPs are certainly reflective, their P preference contributes an impulsive element that may at times diminish or override their introverted reflectiveness.

Extraverts in general, and EPs in particular, are less concerned about committing errors. Their strategy is one of quantity over quality. So rather than taking time to prepare and focus on hitting the target, they simply increase their number of attempts. Whether spending money, promoting a new idea, pursuing a new love interest, or having children, extraverts are generally less cautious and conservative by nature. They are more willing to take risks and "put themselves out there," taking an "act now, think later" sort of approach. While EJs are typically quicker to act than introverts, their J preference contributes a penchant for planning that may in some ways counteract their extraverted quickness.

Strangers (I) vs. Citizens (E) of the World

Introverts typically prefer a quieter, slower-paced lifestyle. They don't particularly enjoy or feel comfortable with the extraverted rat race. There are two interrelated reasons for this. First, as we will soon discuss in greater detail, introverts are more easily overwhelmed by external stimuli. They tend to be more sensitive than extraverts, which can dispose them to feeling anxious or overtaxed when too much is happening around them. Second, introverts prefer a slower and quieter life because it affords them time and space to nourish and replenish themselves. Down time is like air for introverts. They need ample time to catch their breath, reflect on life, and explore their own interests.

Extraverts, by contrast, are more at home in, and energized by the world. Being alone for too long can be unsettling for extraverts, engendering feelings of boredom, restlessness, loneliness, low self-esteem, etc. Extraverts actually feel safer and more comfortable when their attention and energies are directed outwardly. This helps them forget themselves and act without self-consciousness. Introverts, of course, are the opposite. They feel most themselves when "doing their own thing" and more self-conscious when around others.

Sensitive (I) vs. Uninhibited (E)

Why are introverts more careful, cautious, and self-contained than extraverts? Why are they more easily overwhelmed by external demands or stimuli?

For answers to these questions, we will now take a brief detour to explore Jerome Kagan's research on temperament, as well as Elaine Aron's work on "highly sensitive persons."

Kagan is widely recognized for his work on the physiological basis of temperament. In his book, *Galen's Prophecy*, he details a number of studies designed to examine temperamental differences among infants and children.

Kagan found that some infants were more sensitive, anxious, and vigorous in their responses to external stimuli; he referred to these as *high reactives*. Infants who were characteristically calmer and less fearful were classified as *low reactives*. Kagan also studied the characteristics of children and again identified two distinct groups: *inhibited children and uninhibited children*. Inhibited children, according to Kagan, displayed the following characteristics:

- Reluctance to spontaneously engage with unfamiliar children
- Absence of spontaneous smiles with unfamiliar people
- Required more time to relax in new situations
- Reluctance to take risks; cautious behavior
- Unusual fears and phobias
- Heightened muscle tension

In considering these findings, you may have noticed some striking similarities among high-reactive infants, inhibited children, and what we consider introverted characteristics. Kagan noted these associations as well, so he decided to follow his subjects over time to see how inborn temperament might translate into personality. In general, he found that high-reactive infants and inhibited children continued to display introverted characteristics, whereas low reactives and uninhibited children proceeded along a more extraverted path.

Kagan's research dovetails nicely with that of another important theorist, Elaine Aron. Aron is well-known, especially among introverts, for her work on "highly sensitive persons" (HSPs). According to Aron, sensitive individuals are "easily overwhelmed by highly stimulating or unfamiliar situations." Consistent with Kagan's research, she reports that approximately 70% of sensitive persons are introverted.

The work of Kagan and Aron provides a helpful starting point for decoding the psychophysiological differences between introverts and extraverts. Even at birth, fledgling introverts tend to be more fearful, reactive, and guarded. They seem to experience the world as a precarious place, one that requires vigilance to ensure their safety and survival. Being more sensitive and prone to hyperarousal, they naturally seek time alone, finding safety and comfort in their own corner of the world. Even as adults, introverts take measures to protect themselves against unwanted intrusions, maintaining a line of separation between themselves and the world.

Like Kagan's low-reactive infants and uninhibited children, extraverts tend to be less sensitive and less intimidated by external stimuli. This grants them more confidence to boldly move outward and explore the world directly, spawning their development as "citizens of the world."

A Mixed Bag

As discussed at the outset of this book, we all have a fixed and stable personality type. We are either introverts or extraverts. At our core, none of us are ambiverts. This does not mean, however, that we all present as extreme introverts or extraverts. Indeed, many of us look more like a mixed bag of E and I.

In thinking about the E-I preference, it is helpful to keep in mind that all extraverts have introverted auxiliary and inferior functions, which means they will display some degree of inner concern and focus. Similarly, introverts' use of extraverted auxiliary and inferior functions may compel them to (eventually) make their mark on the world at large.

The drive for personal growth can also lead to a mixing of E and I tendencies. Namely, for introverts, personal growth involves "taking the inside (I) out (E)," which may inspire them to direct more of their attention and energy outwardly. For extraverts, personal growth entails "bringing the outside (E) in (I)," which may contribute to an increasingly inward focus.

Since so many things in life demand a measure of extraversion, introverts seem particularly obligated and likely to develop their extraverted capacities. It is difficult, after all, to survive school, family, work, or peer interactions without some degree of extraverted development. While not necessarily a bad thing, this may at times make it more difficult for introverts to recognize their E-I preference.

Other personality preferences and functions can also cloud our E-I preference. Consider, for instance, the issue of talkativeness. While most folks assume extraverts to be more talkative than introverts, there are other preferences, as well as functions, that factor into talkativeness. Generally speaking, the E, N, and J preferences can be associated with higher levels of talkativeness, as can the function,

Extraverted Feeling (Fe). It would therefore not be unusual, for instance, to find an INFJ more loquacious than an ESTP.

We can see from this example how tricky typing can be. If we were to use talkativeness as our sole E-I criterion, then INFJs and ESTPs, as well as other types, might regularly misidentify their true preference. This reminds us of the importance of considering the bigger picture, of taking a bird'seye view, as you go about discerning your personality preferences.

Summary

Common Introverted Traits:

- Inner/self-focus

- More independent-minded

- More cautious, conservative, and discriminating; "look before they leap"; rely heavily on forethought (especially IJs)

- Prefer a slower, quieter, reflective life

- More easily overwhelmed by external stimuli

- Feel somewhat alien, uncomfortable, or inadequate in the world

- Often less talkative (especially ISPs)

- More self-reflective and self-aware

- Require more time to themselves

Common Extraverted Traits:

- Outer/world-focus

- More collective-minded

- "Act now, think later" (especially EPs); more assertive and risk-tolerant

- Enjoy a busier, "on the go" lifestyle
- Less concerned with being harmed or overwhelmed by world
- Feel rather at home in the world
- Often more talkative (especially ENJs)
- More world-reflective and world-aware
- Require less time to themselves

Common E-I Mistypings

Having now developed a working understanding of introversion and extraversion, I'd like to take a moment to consider some common E-I mistypings; that is, when introverts misclassify themselves as extraverts or vice-versa.

As is true of the other preferences, one of the most common reasons for E-I mistypings is the inferior function. Because introverts' inferior function is extraverted in nature, they have a desire to "turn their insides out." Not only may this compel them to strive after fame, influence, or status, but it may also lead them to mistype as extraverts. Similarly, extraverts, in striving to "turn their outsides in," to know or better themselves, may mistype as introverts.

E-I mistypings can also stem from J-P issues. Namely, because perceivers are more impulsive and less careful than judgers, IPs may mistake themselves for extraverts. Similarly, since judging types tend to be more careful, cautious, and deliberative, EJs may mistype as introverts.

Another common mistyping involves ENPs misclassifying as INPs. Since ENPs are strong intuitives, they may confuse being intuitive with being introverted, since both I and N can be associated with reflectiveness. ENPs may also be less physically active than other extraverts, since it is really their mind that is most actively engaging with the world. So while their attention is still outwardly directed, the predominantly mental nature of their extraversion may serve as a point of confusion.

Our final E-I mistyping involves ISPs, who may misclassify as extraverts because of their tendency to function as "busy bodies." They may mistakenly assume that, because extraverts lead an active lifestyle, their penchant for being busy and active suggests they are extraverts. This mistyping represents the flip side of what we saw with ENPs, who are prone to conflating higher levels of mental activity with introversion.

This concludes our analysis of the E-I preference. For those seeking a more extensive look at introverts and extraverts, I recommend Susan Cain's excellent book, *Quiet: The Power of Introverts in a World that Can't Stop Talking.*

Chapter 4

SENSING (S) vs.
INTUITION (N)

In its broadest sense, the S-N dimension can be seen as corresponding to philosophical notions of material (S) and immaterial (N), seen (S) and unseen (N), empirical (S) and theoretical (N), matter (S) and mind (N), physics (S) and metaphysics (N).

According to Jung, sensing and intuition are perceiving functions, responsible for receiving or retrieving information. Watching television, smelling flowers, reading novels, and recalling something from memory are examples of perceiving activities. Unlike the judging functions, which often involve a sense of volition and intentionality, the perceiving functions typically feel more passive in nature, as the vast majority of our perceptions are handled automatically and subconsciously.

Of the two modes of perceiving, sensing is easier for most people to comprehend. After all, most of us are familiar with the "five senses"— sight, smell, taste, hearing, and touch. The notion of intuition, however, seems more vague and esoteric. We must therefore take a closer look at intuition, as well as how it compares and contrasts with sensing.

What Exactly is Intuition?

While our senses tell us about the surface appearance of things, intuition dives deeper, discerning hidden patterns, connections, and motivations. It surveys available information, both conscious and unconscious, and works to get a sense of what things mean or look like when taken as a whole. It excels at making inferences, filling in any holes or gaps to develop theories and explanations.

When dominant intuitives (i.e., INJs and ENPs) express the need to "think about" something, this means something quite different from what it might for other types. Namely, the lion's share of their thinking occurs subconsciously, outside the bounds of conscious control and awareness. Consequently, their ideas and insights often arrive unexpectedly, as if coming from "out of the blue." In his bestselling book, Blink, Malcolm Gladwell cleverly describes intuition as "thinking without thinking." For intuitives, "sleeping on a problem" is as sure a route to a solution as any.

Because the products of intuition are commonly experienced as unexpected gifts, its workings are sometimes perceived as magical or mystical. But thanks to Jung and company, we can now identify the magician as the subconscious mind. Enjoying ready access to the ideational magician that is the subconscious, intuitives have a knack for generating and working with ideas, associations, theories, symbols, and other abstractions.

Although intuitives are privy to subconscious ideas and images, there is still a sense in which they cannot control the creative process. What they can control, at least to some extent, is what they do with their conscious mind. Namely, they can control the types of information they ingest, as well as the sorts of questions or problems they consciously (and therefore also subconsciously) wrestle with. The more they immerse themselves in a certain topic or interest area, the more their subconscious will eventually yield.

As strange as it might seem from a sensor's perspective, the concrete world is not what is most "real" for intuitives (especially for ENPs and INJs). It is not the physical realm, but the metaphysical realm, that constitutes their primary reality. Indeed, many intuitives have a weak sense of connection to the physical world, even to their own bodies. Some report feelings of disembodiment or a lingering sense of déjà vu. Because of their close kinship with the subconscious, their routine existence can assume a dreamlike or abstracted quality, blurring the distinction between dreams and reality. This is why intuitives are often well-described as dreamy, absent-minded, oblivious, or otherworldly.

"All on the Table"

To further illustrate S-N differences, let's briefly turn our attention to the exciting world of tables. Yes, I did say tables, you know those things with flat tops and four legs.

We all know that a table has specific parts and features—its size, shape, contours, texture, color, and constitutive materials. Such are its sensing-related elements.

But there is a more to a table than what meets the eye (or the hands). A table is also an idea, a concept, a mental image. This aspect of the table is handled by intuition.

We also know that there are different types of tables. Indeed, there is an infinite number of potential tables. But at the end of the day, they are all still tables. This shows us that we have a foundational idea of what a table is (Ni), as well as the capacity to envision different types of tables (Ne).

In light of the above, tables can teach us about the differences between sensing and intuition, as well as how they work together in a complementary fashion. Clearly, both S and N are essential to our ability to create and recognize tables. Without the idea (N) of a table, we would have no point of reference for identifying or constructing a table. Likewise, without the materials and physical labor (S), the table would remain but an unrealized idea.

Potential (N) vs. Actual (S)

Just as intuition gives us ideas about things like tables, intuitives are "idea people." They work on the front end, so to speak, of the creative process. They, or perhaps more accurately, their subconscious minds, create or bring forth potentials in the form of ideas or images (e.g., envisioning a new type of table). Sensing types, by contrast, are wired to work on the back end of the creative process. It is their role to enact and actualize, to give physical form to, ideas and potentials. They are the hands, feet, and senses of the creative process.

Since intuitives are inclined to work with ideas, theories, and mental imagery, they spend ample time contemplating life in abstract ways. They enjoy peering beneath the surface to see how things (or people) work, as well as how they are connected and interrelated. They enjoy lengthy discussions of abstract matters like theology, philosophy, political theory, science, and so on. They tend to feel more comfortable observing and appraising life from afar than diving in and getting their hands dirty. For intuitives, spending time in thought and the imagination comes more naturally than doing, acting, or implementing. Dominant intuitives (ENPs and INJs), in particular, may lack confidence in their ability to materialize their ideas or to handle S details. They may worry that their actions or creations will fail to measure up to their imagined ideals, that actuality will fall short of potentiality.

Sensing types, by contrast, may furtively fret about their ability to produce good ideas or theories. For instance, an ESFP friend of mine recently apprised me of her concerns about finishing a 10-page paper in a month's time. Since N is her inferior and therefore least accessible function, it is not surprising that she lacks confidence in generating and stringing together ideas. While intuitive types often enjoy abstract challenges such as writing term papers, sensing types like my friend are more apt to enjoy concrete activities, such as laboratory sessions or field experiences.

Another great example of S-N differences can be gleaned from the world of music. While some musicians may excel in both music composition and performance, this is the exception rather than the rule. Indeed, this is why music education programs are commonly divided into two separate tracks: a theory / composition (N) track and a performance (S) track. N musicians typically excel and take interest in the front end of a musical production, composing nuanced, intricate, and thoughtful songs. The strength of S musicians, by contrast, is usually on the back end. Whether singing, dancing, or playing instruments, they are naturals when it comes to execution and performance (especially SPs).

Connections (N) vs. Particulars (S)

Intuition is a synthesizing and associating function. It is concerned with how things connect and relate to each other. It is particularly interested in relationships among ideas, in seeing connections between one abstraction and another. Intuitives are more interested in the connections between things than they are in the things themselves. This includes identifying patterns of causal relations and developing explanatory theories.

Sensing types, by contrast, tend to focus more on details and particulars than on the way things connect up. In having a less intimate connection with the ideational subconscious, they are less attuned to hidden patterns and underlying relationships. While certainly aware of overt physical laws, they are less inclined to spend time reflecting on deeper causes and abstract theories. This is especially true for S dominants (ISJs and ESPs), for whom N is inferior.

In like fashion, intuitives, especially ENPs and INJs, may struggle when it comes to handling S details. Since their minds are often engrossed in abstractions, they may fail to see things that are right under their noses. They may lose track of time, forget to pay the bills, misplace their keys, skip over buttons and belt loops, fail to balance the checkbook, etc. In light of their shortcomings with respect to everyday details, they are often well described as oblivious or absent-minded.

Summary

Characteristics of Sensors:

- Caught up in living life, they may forget to reflect on it (especially ESPs)
- Generally prefer and are at their best with practical, concrete activities
- Excel in handling details and daily affairs
- Lovers of new sights, tastes, and sensations (SPs) or routines and traditions (SJs)
- More concerned with the facts, details, or particulars than the connections between them
- Most effective on the back end of the creative process, with enacting and implementing

Characteristics of Intuitives:

- Often lost in thought, their minds are "somewhere else"
- May struggle to attend to the concrete details of daily life (especially INJs and ENPs)
- Prefer to deal in theoretical, imaginative, or speculative realms; love working with ideas

- Enjoy contemplating abstract patterns, connections, and languages, be they verbal, mathematical, or computer-based
- More interested in the connections between things (especially abstract things) than in the things themselves
- Most effective on the front end of the creative process, with generating ideas or insights

Common S-N Mistypings

As we saw with the E-I dimension, there are certain situations in which sensors commonly mistype as intuitives, and vice-versa. On the whole, however, it seems more common for sensors to mistype as intuitives than the other way around.

One common mistyping involves IS types misidentifying as intuitives. This relates to the fact that both introversion and intuition contribute an element of reflectiveness. ISPs may be particularly prone to S-N errors, since neither sensing nor intuition serves as their dominant function.

As with the other personality preferences, the inferior function is another common culprit in S-N mistypings. Specifically, ESPs striving after the wisdom and insight promised by their inferior Ni may be prone to mistype as intuitives. Similarly, ISJs desirous of Ne cleverness and creativity may misidentify as INJs. While ENPs and INJs seem less likely to mistype as sensors, for those who do, the inferior function is often at play.

Last, associating intuition with open-mindedness or certain types of intelligence may inspire sensors to mistype as intuitives. This seems especially likely for sensors with higher IQs.

Chapter 5

THINKING (T) vs. FEELING (F)

On a broad level, thinking and feeling point to what are commonly conceived as masculine (T) - feminine (F) differences. While not synonymous with sex differences, demographic data support the common observation that the majority of males prefer thinking and females feeling.

Because of its association with masculinity and femininity, the T-F dichotomy seems to be one of the easiest for people to comprehend. This of course is not to say we all have an easy time deciphering our T-F preference, especially those sporting a more androgynous personality. EPs and IJs may find discerning their T-F preference particularly challenging, since neither thinking nor feeling serves as their dominant function.

Jung classified thinking and feeling as judging functions. They are in charge of evaluating information, making decisions, and drawing conclusions.

The primary difference between thinking judgments and feeling judgments is the nature of their evaluative criteria. As we will see, thinkers tend to use impersonal, logic-based criteria, while feelers consider tastes and feelings—both their own and those of others—in making decisions.

Thinkers and feelers also differ in their areas of interest and expertise. Typically, these are directly related to their preferred judging criteria. Namely, thinkers tend to take interest in activities requiring the application of impersonal logic, while feelers take up pursuits that draw on their tastes, feelings, and people-related concerns.

As with the other preferences, it's not that thinkers never have feelings or that feelers never use logic. Rather, they differ in the degree to which they lead with logic versus tastes and feelings; this is why we describe T and F as *preferences*.

Overview of Thinking

Thinking judgments are logic-based. This is why thinkers tend to excel and take interest in fields requiring logical or strategical thinking such as the sciences, mathematics, philosophy, computer science, business, or engineering. Even those involved in F-related fields, such as healthcare, tend to work their way into T niches, such as research, informatics, operations management, and the like.

Thinking has a quantitative bent to it; it is a "calculating" function. Even if subconsciously, it is constantly weighing odds and scheming ways of moving things in a better direction. Such calculations play an important role in strategical and logistical thinking, computing ways of reducing costs or improving efficiency and productivity.

Systematizing and classifying also factor into the thinker's arsenal, especially that of NTs. Scientists and philosophers alike display a penchant for ordering and systematizing information. NTJs, in particular, are commonly described as "systems thinkers." This involves seeing the world as a giant system composed of myriad subsystems, each of which can be analyzed and rationally explicated.

Thinkers also tend to experience diminished emotional responses, at least compared to those of their feeling counterparts. They generally show less interest in and concern for their own feelings, as well as those of others. After all, the reason thinking and feeling have long been conceived of as opposites is because logic-based processing and emotion-based processing cannot occur simultaneously. This is not to say that thinkers and feelers never arrive at similar conclusions or come to a point of mutual understanding; nor is it to say than an individual cannot alternate between these two modes of processing, considering things from both T and F vantage points. The point is simply that thinking and feeling use very different evaluative mechanisms and criteria, which makes it difficult for them to operate simultaneously, or *co-operate* if you will.

Since their feelings are typically confined to the backstage of their consciousness, thinkers are sometimes conceived as emotionally distant or detached. While not always beneficial for their relationships, emotional detachment can be advantageous for effective logical processing. This is not to say that thinkers should avoid feeling-related matters, but there are times when unalloyed logical processing proves useful.

Because thinkers spend less time attuning to and meeting the needs of others, they have more time and energy to devote to their work. Indeed, for many thinkers, their work is the central focus of their lives. Just as feelers often aspire to help others or strengthen their relationships, thinkers strive to advance in their work. To be clear, it's not that feelers don't also aspire toward or achieve excellence in their interest areas. But in many cases, their attention and energies are divided among work, relationships, and caregiving. Thinkers, especially thinking-dominant (ITPs and ETJs) males, tend to be more one-track minded, granting their work the lion's share of their attention and devotion.

Overview of Feeling

The feeling function weighs and evaluates our affective responses to the world. Not only are feelers aware of their emotions, but they are also attuned to emotional nuances and subtleties (just as thinkers are attuned to logical subtleties). Indeed, for every emotion in a thinker's arsenal, a feeler may distinguish a multitude of feelings or feeling tones.

Because feelers discern a greater breadth of emotional variations and nuances, they may feel that words are inadequate to capture and convey their experiences. Many turn to poetry, music, fashion, or the arts as avenues for evoking, exploring, refining, or expressing their complex and nuanced emotions. Feeling also pertains to the development and refinement of tastes, which is another reason feelers are drawn to the arts.

If we associate thinking with black-and-white, logical criteria, then feeling can be viewed to involve a more colorful, qualitative approach. While thinking focuses on things like technology and functionality, feeling strives to enhance our lives in less "functional" or "practical" ways. It embellishes, enlivens, and enriches with color, feeling, and style.

Feelers also have a propensity to function as nurturers and caregivers. They can often be found caring for children, plants, animals, family members, employees, and the underserved. They serve as a sort of social glue that keeps people healthy, connected, and attuned to each other's needs and feelings. While female feelers tend to be the most nurturing of all types, male feelers are also quite nurturing. Male nurses, therapists, and flight attendants, for instance, are commonly feeling types.

It's important to recognize that feeling should not be equated with irrationality. Indeed, Jung went out of his way to ensure that thinking and feeling were approached on equal grounds, classifying both as "rational" functions. Jung also took care to distinguish the feeling function from emotions, essentially saying that the feeling function is charged with evaluating emotions. From a practical standpoint, however, the fact remains that feelers must navigate a world of ever-changing emotions. And in my view, feelings and emotions are entirely reasonable and useful tools for navigating human affairs. Just as certain types of logic or formulae are appropriate for solving logic-based problems, emotions are appropriate, even necessary, for addressing a spectrum of human problems and needs. The very notion of emotional intelligence speaks to the value of experiencing, understanding, and communicating the important truths and qualities conveyed through feelings.

Taste & Style: S, F, or Both?

In light of my assertion that feelers bring taste, color, and style to the world, you may be wondering where feeling ends and sensing begins.

On a theoretical level, it is tempting to suggest that the feeling preference is unrelated to taste, style, and fashion. From an empirical perspective, however, this seems unacceptable, given that feeling types typically display stronger interests in the arts, fashion, scents, cooking, and so on. Even NF writers (e.g., novelists) tend to include much in the way of sensory detail in their works. This is suggestive of a connection between sensations and emotions, which leads me to believe that taste, style, and fashion pertain to both the S and F preferences.

As a counterpoint to this, one could argue that thinkers have their own sense of taste and style, even if focused more on things like functionality and efficiency. But even then, the fact remains that thinkers are less interested in thinking about styles and fashions than other matters. This reminds us of the different evaluative criteria employed by thinkers and feelers. Namely, thinkers don't invest a lot of time judging fashions and styles because these things fall outside the purview of logic. Likewise, feelers tend not to obsess over solving logical problems that fall beyond the evaluative scope of feeling.

In positing some degree of SF overlap with respect to the notions of taste and style, I am in no way suggesting this as a barrier to effective typing. There are plenty of other criteria, discussed in this chapter and others, that can be used for the sake of T-F, as well as S-N, clarification.

What about Values?

It is commonplace in typological circles to associate the feeling preference with a concern for "values." In light of the similarity of preferences and values (i.e., we prefer what we value, and value what we prefer), this can appear a bit problematic. After all, T and F (as well as S and N) are preferences, and could even by construed as values, at least in a general sense.

The real difference between thinkers and feelers involves *what* they value. As we've seen, thinkers value improving the functionality of things. They value things like efficiency, utility, and good strategy. Feelers, on the other hand, value the way things look, smell, taste, and sound, all of which impact their feelings. Feelers also place higher value on people and relationships, while being more sensitive to perceived instances of injustice, inequality, and other moral issues.

When typologists associate values with F, my sense is that the term is typically being used in a moral or people-related sense (e.g., family or humanitarian values). This is generally an accurate attribution, since thinkers tend to be more concerned about themselves or their work than the well-being of others. With that said, using the term "values" without further qualification may at times be misleading, since thinkers value T matters to the same degree that feelers value F matters.

T-F & Gender

To some extent, I feel sorry for male feelers and female thinkers trying to understanding themselves through the lens of typology. After all, the vast majority of type profiles are written with a particular sex in mind. Thinking profiles are often written with men in mind and feeling profiles with women in mind. This can make it challenging for T females and F males to feel confident about their personality type.

Part of the problem is that, even when type is accounted for, gender still contributes to personality differences. A 2001 paper entitled, "Gender Differences in Personality Traits Across Cultures," found consistent gender differences across 26 cultures (Costa, et al.). Most notable for our purposes, this study showed that women are generally more nurturing than men. Even the issuers of the MBTI are aware of the impact of gender, evidenced by the fact that the MBTI factors gender into its T-F tabulations.

A more recent study (2013), "Sex Differences in the Structural Connectome of the Human Brain," revealed that female brains display greater neuronal connectivity between hemispheres, whereas male brains show increased connectivity within each hemisphere. In interpreting these findings, the researchers suggested that females are more likely to integrate right (e.g., intuitive, emotional) and left-brained (analytical) styles in their processing, while males will tend to show less integration. If we apply these findings typologically, we might expect males of all types to experience a greater gulf between thinking and feeling than their female counterparts. If this is the case, it would further support the notion that thinking males are more apt to display extreme T characteristics (e.g., autism) than thinking females. These findings might also predict females to experience greater difficulty sorting out their T-F preference due to greater communication and overlap between brain hemispheres.

In light of these studies, if you are on the fence between T and F, it appears warranted to compare your personality with the typical T-F presentation of your own gender. Thoroughly exploring the specific T and F functions (Ti, Te, Fi, Fe) will also help you clarify your T-F preference.

Summary

Characteristics of Thinkers:

- Take a logic-based approach to reasoning and decision-making
- Focus on matters of logic, strategy, logistics, utility, functionality, and classification; strive to make things more useful, rational, and efficient
- More readily detach from their emotions to make decisions in an impersonal fashion
- Less concerned with the needs and feelings of others
- Focus more on their own work and interests

Characteristics of Feelers:

- Consult tastes and feelings in reasoning and decision-making
- Enrich life with colors, sounds, tastes, scents, textures, stories, images, etc.
- More attuned and responsive to feelings, both their own and those of others
- Generally more caring, compassionate, and nurturing
- More apt to divide time among work, relationships, and/or caregiving

Among the more prominent causes of T-F confusion is gender, which we just finished discussing. Another common cause is the inferior function. ETJs or ITPs caught up in a whirlwind romance, for instance, may be prone to identifying with their inferior feeling function. Similarly, IFPs or EFJs studying math, engineering, or other

T subjects may over-identify with their inferior thinking function. In such instances, once the inferior function need has been sufficiently quelled or exhausted (e.g., when a thinker gets married or a feeler fatigues of T-related work), the focus naturally reverts back to the dominant function and the individual realizes his or her typing error.

EPs and IJs are also prone to struggle with their T-F designation. One reason for this is neither IJs nor EPs use thinking or feeling as their dominant function. Hence, they are really working to identify their auxiliary function. Identifying the auxiliary can be more difficult, especially early in life, when it has yet to be fully explored or developed.

More specifically, IFJs are apt to mistype as thinkers and ETPs as feelers. This is because the I, T, and J preferences are all roughly associated with the left side of the brain, so if exhibiting a more left-brained style, IFJs (especially ISFJs) may mistype as thinkers. Similarly, the E, F, and P preferences have often been associated with the right hemisphere, so in displaying a more right-brained style, ETPs may misidentify as feelers. It is therefore particularly important that IJs and EPs be capable of differentiating the various T and F functions (Ti, Te, Fi, Fe) in order to accurately identify their T-F preference.

Chapter 6

JUDGING (J) vs. PERCEIVING (P)

In the broadest sense, perceiving refers to the act of taking in information (i.e., *information collecting*), while judging describes the process of making judgments and discriminations (i.e., *information evaluating*). Both processes are readily observable outside of human affairs, with even the most rudimentary organisms exhibiting stimulus (P)-response (J) mechanisms. Judging and perceiving also correspond to notions of static (J) versus dynamic (P) scientific and philosophical models. Philosophers have long debated whether ultimate reality is static and unchanging (J) or forever in flux (P). Similarly, physicists have toiled to determine whether physical reality is composed of waves (P) or particles (J).

Jung did not use the J-P label to describe the types. The J-P indicator was added later by Myers and Briggs. As we saw in the Introduction, it is largely concerned with outward behavior and attitudes. More specifically, it indicates whether the first extraverted function in a type's functional stack is an extraverted judging function (i.e., Fe or Te) or an extraverted perceiving function (i.e., Ne or Se). This approach is rather straightforward for extraverts, since their first extraverted function also happens to be their dominant function. There is no confusion, for instance, in calling an ENFP a perceiver or an ENTJ a judger, since this accurately portrays the dominant mode of operation for these types.

For introverted types, however, J and P can be a source of confusion and misunderstanding. This is due to the fact that introverts' first extraverted function is *auxiliary* rather than dominant. Consequently, the J-P designation of IPs and IJs does not describe the nature of their dominant function. As strange as it may sound, IPs' preferred and dominant mode of functioning is judging (Fi or Ti) and IJs' is perceiving (Si or Ni).

Making matters worse, there is a fair amount of misinformation regarding what constitutes J-P characteristics. Some typology authors or websites, for instance, make claims like: "P types are messy, disorganized, procrastinators, and chronically late." Or, "J types are neat, tidy, organized, and uptight." We can understand the origins of these assumptions if we think of judging as "static and predictable" and perceiving as "fluid and unpredictable." Unfortunately, these things rarely play out so neatly in reality. There are simply too many confounding variables involved.

In light of this, it appears we have our work cut out for us with respect to clarifying the core characteristics of Js and Ps. Before diving into the specifics, however, I would like to start with broad overviews of Js and Ps, giving due emphasis to their outer presentation:

J types are outwardly firm, direct, and opinionated. They are more inclined to directly express their views and wishes by way of declarative statements (e.g., "I feel that…" or "I don't like…"or "We should…"). Hence, others often turn to them in situations requiring a firm decision or answer. This contributes to their status as potential leaders, teachers, or managers. Their tone and mannerisms also convey a sense of closure that may cause them to appear more formal or serious in their presentation. Despite what many type descriptions may suggest, they are not necessarily neat, tidy, organized, uptight, or punctual.

P types, by contrast, are outwardly open, receptive, and adaptable. They are less apt to declare their opinions or impose their will on others. They tend to express things in an open-ended (e.g., "What do you think about…?") rather than declarative fashion. They are often perceived as good listeners and non-judgmental in their attitude toward others, exuding an air of openness and informality. Contrary to some conceptions, they are not necessarily messy, disorganized, procrastinating, or chronically late.

As a word of warning, there are parts of this chapter that may seem a bit complicated or confusing. But try not to worry. At the end of this chapter, I've included a summary of important J-P characteristics that should give you a good sense of your overall preference. We will also revisit and expound on some of these issues in Chapter 16. As usual, try not to get too hung up on particulars and focus instead on seeing your overall preference. Also, because the J-P preference is based largely on how you present outwardly, you may find it helpful to ask others where they see you on the J-P spectrum.

Structured (J) vs. Unstructured (P)

Judging is often associated with a preference for structure, especially *external* structure. There is some truth to the notion of J types having a stronger preference (or tolerance) for outer structure than P types. Js tend to be more at home, for instance, in structured work environments. P types, by contrast, can feel bored, restless, or stifled when surrounded by too much structure. While Ps don't mind imposing structure on themselves or their surroundings, they dislike feeling controlled or constrained from without.

With that said, a preference for external structure does not necessarily translate into being neat or tidy. I have met plenty of IJs, for example, who show diminished concern or effort with respect to being neat, tidy, or organized. Of all types, ESTJs seem most concerned with being neat and tidy, since an orderly living space can be associated, to some extent, with S (i.e., attention to concrete matters), and to a larger extent, with Te (especially dominant Te).

Planned (J) vs. Open-Ended (P)

The J preference is commonly associated with planning ahead, while Ps prefer to keep things more open-ended. Since planning, by definition, involves reflection before action, introversion may also contribute to a propensity for planning. Hence, IJs are predicted to function as the most careful planners. They are particularly likely to plan (often extensively) for special events involving other people, such as vacations, holidays, birthdays, and so on.

As we will soon discuss, P types can be rather indecisive. And because planning requires that decisions be made in advance, Ps are prone to putting off or even forgoing planning altogether. This is especially true if the event involves other people or falls outside their primary interest area. When confronted by others inquiring about plans, Ps are inclined to think or say things like "We'll figure it out" or "Things will work out one way or another." From this, we see that Ps are more inclined to trust the hands of fate. To a certain extent, they even enjoy not knowing exactly how things will play out. They relish the sense of mystery and excitement toward future unknowns. J types, especially IJs, are apt to see the P-approach as risky, lazy, or foolish. They prefer to spend more time planning on the front-end to avoid potential frustrations and problems on the back-end.

J Types: Conviction & Convergence

J types, by definition, are more outwardly firm and direct in their expressions. They exude a sense of closure in their communication and mannerisms. And while the J-P dimension was originally formulated to reflect a type's outer presentation, in some respects, the inner world of J types is more convergent and crystallized than that of P types.

While SJs and NJs may often conceive of the world quite differently, they are similar in their tendency to see *one view* as more correct, appropriate, or ideal. Unlike Se and Ne (the functions used by SPs and NPs respectively), which are characteristically divergent, open-ended, and undiscriminating, Si and Ni are more convergent, producing what amounts to a singular vision of things.

As we will discuss in future chapters, SJs' Si effectively takes the entirety of an individual's past experiences and condenses them into a limited set of perspectives, habits, and routines. SJs use this condensed past as a blueprint for informing present and future behavior. NJs' Ni also functions convergently, subconsciously synthesizing information to produce insights, answers, and explanations. The inner clarity and convergence of Si and Ni beget greater consistency and predictability (J) in both thought and action.

Since their ideation is less susceptible to significant perturbations or fluctuations, J types seem to have an easier time drawing firm conclusions about their personality type. They are also less sensitive to, or concerned with, potential exceptions to their beliefs and worldview. While P types may be rattled by a single exception or contradiction, J types are typically more resilient and steadfast in their convictions.

P Types: Exploring & Experimenting

P types, especially NPs, find it difficult not to see things as grey or ambiguous, including their personality type, career path, relationships, etc. For NPs, this can be attributed to their Ne function, which specializes in injecting uncertainty into things. Ne sees multiple explanations and possibilities for nearly anything. Consequently, privileging a single vision or version of reality can prove difficult for

NPs, especially in the first half of life. They are your quintessential *seekers*, *explorers*, and *wanderers*.

SPs also exhibit diminished convergence and conviction compared to their SJ counterparts. While SPs may not fluctuate philosophically in the way of NPs, they may show significant uncertainty with respect to practical matters, such as finding the right career or romantic partner.

The primary means by which P types move toward convergence is trial-and-error experimentation. This may involve exploring new ideas, experiences, or possibilities. P types need ample time to explore and experiment before they can reach anything resembling a sense of closure.

From the J perspective, Ps may appear like rats in a maze, blindly exploring all the different pathways and frequently encountering dead-ends. As we saw earlier, IJs, in particular, feel that greater foresight obviates the need for excessive experimentation or risk-taking. *But P types tend to lack confidence in foresight.* NPs, in particular, may foresee many options, but lack the discrimination or sense of inner conviction to know which is best. They therefore feel it necessary to explore and experiment with all the options (i.e., exhausting all the "dead-ends") in order to make their way through the maze and reach a point of closure.

Seeking vs. Experiencing Closure

It is often said that J types prefer closure. This notion may derive from their tendency to plan ahead, as well as from the firm and direct nature of their expressions. And while it is generally true that J types *experience* more closure and convergence in their beliefs (see above), it is inaccurate to suggest that all J types *seek* closure in their beliefs.

It is primarily EJs, not so much IJs, who can be understood as seeking closure in their beliefs. Since IJs' dominant function (Si or Ni) is a perceiving function, it seems somewhat contradictory to suggest that IJs are preoccupied with closure, at least not inwardly. As inner perceivers, IJs are actually far more leisurely and easygoing inwardly than they may appear outwardly.

In light of the fact that the judging functions are charged with decision-making and can thereby be seen as "seeking closure," it stands to reason that types with a dominant judging function (i.e., IPs and EJs) would be the most preoccupied with seeking closure or convergence. This, combined with our earlier discussion of Js experiencing closure, leads to the following suppositions:

- EJs actively seek and readily experience closure
- EPs neither strongly seek nor readily experience closure
- IJs experience, but do not strongly seek, closure
- IPs seek, but do not readily experience, closure

This illustrates a point we will further discuss in Chapter 16, which is that EPs are well understood as the "purest" perceivers and EJs as the "purest" judgers. IJs and IPs, however, are more of a complicated mixture of J and P characteristics. IJs are more open and easygoing inwardly than they let on outwardly, while IPs' outer adaptability belies their inner seriousness and intentionality.

The Laws of Js & Ps

We often think of J types as the "lawmakers." This is largely due to the fact that their judging function (Te or Fe) is extraverted. In being more concerned with outer order and structure, they are more prone to creating and enforcing collective laws and standards. SJs, in particular, may display an authoritarian bent, feeling that people should "fall in line" and "obey the rules."

It may come as a surprise then to hear that P types are equally disposed to lawmaking. They differ from Js, however, with respect to the target and direction of their lawmaking efforts. Namely, P laws, created and instituted by Fi or Ti, are introverted in their direction and focus. They are concerned with regulating and directing the self and its activities. Hence, Ps can be seen as living according to their own inner rules and dictates. They are naturally averse to external rules and directives, with TPs being most repelled by Te rules (e.g., organizational rules, "red tape") and FPs by Fe rules (e.g., various social norms and conventions). Being told what to do or how to do something, particularly when unsolicited, can feel repulsive to them (e.g., "How dare you tell me what to do or presume to know what is best for me!"). This is particularly true for IPs, whose inner law-making function (Fi or Ti) is dominant. In light of their aversion to collective rules, P types are often viewed as more rebellious and unconventional (especially NPs). They inject chaos into J attempts at outer order and cohesiveness.

Unlike J laws, which are externally directed and therefore readily revealed, P laws are often concealed from the outside observer. So unless you happen to be the P who crafted the law, you may never get a clear sense of what it is. You may be able to make inferences about it, based on behavioral or other clues, but outside of a concerted attempt to inquire into it, it may remain rather inscrutable.

In light of the above, it is not surprising that Ps and Js are susceptible to misunderstandings and conflicts of interest. Like introverts, Ps can be staunch defenders of individual liberties. They fight to ensure that outer J laws do not impinge on their personal freedom. J types, on the other hand, are more apt to emphasize collective duty and responsibility. EJs are particularly likely to put collective laws before personal ones, working to ensure that individual freedoms don't compromise collective order.

Are J Types More Responsible? Moral?

Another common belief is that J types are more dutiful and responsible than P types. Once again, this supposition is founded on the extraverted nature of their J function, which makes their dutifulness and devotion more overt. But if Ps create laws to the same extent as Js, might they not also be equally dutiful and responsible? After all, why would Ps create laws for themselves if they had no intention of following them? I suggest Ps are indeed equally dutiful and responsible as J types. The difference is Ps are dutiful and responsible with respect to themselves, to their own rules and principles, rather than to collective standards (here again, we see some similarities between introverts and perceivers).

This issue cuts right to the heart of typological and moral theory. Namely, for P types, there is the sense that morality is not based on following laws "out there," but following laws "in here." From the J perspective, Ps acting according to an unseen inner law might be viewed as acting immorally, especially if the P law contradicts an existing outer law. From the P perspective, however, she is acting dutifully and responsibly according to her own inner dictates.

This is not to say that J types don't also have an inner moral compass. But the fact remains that Js' primary judging function (Fe or Te) is directed outwardly, whereas Ps' (Ti or Fi) is self-referencing. These differences are most clearly evidenced when comparing EJs and IPs.

Restlessness & Breadth of Activities

As inner perceivers (Si or Ni), IJs are the least dependent of all types on outside stimulation. They can sit for hours in one place without feeling restless or compelled to change activities. Because they are less impulsive and their perceptions are more convergent, they tend to be less restless—both mentally and physically.

P types, by contrast, are more restless, impulsive, and divergent in their perceptions. They are stimulated by a breadth of external input, be it through Ne or Se. They find it harder to stay perched in one place before getting the itch to do something else (especially EPs). They seem to need more diversity in their activities to remain engaged and stimulated. In this sense, there may be something to the notion of Ps being more fluid and changeable, since their restlessness often demands it.

J-P & Work

Our J-P preference also affects the type of work and workplace we prefer. We've already discussed how Js are more inclined to feel comfortable in structured environments, preferring more consistency or predictability in their surroundings. Too much external change or chaos may force J types to use extraverted perceiving rather than their preferred mode of introverted perceiving. P types, by contrast, are stimulated by outer change and diversity. Settings that are too static or sterile can feel stifling and uninspiring to them.

Our next consideration is what types of work are most optimal and fulfilling for Js and Ps. Since the J mind is more convergent in nature, it is better suited for work requiring the development of convergent solutions (NJs), following specific policies and protocols (SJs), or managing / advising / teaching. A central work activity for NJs is analysis, whether involving human (NFJs) or non-human systems (NTJs). For SJs, working according to pre-established guidelines is desirable.

The P mind, as we've seen, is more divergent, making it well-suited for a variety of work activities, including opportunities to function creatively or spontaneously. For NPs, a key work activity is divergent thinking. For NFPs, this may involve working as writers, musicians, designers, or artists, while NTPs may find creative outlets in fields like engineering, non-fiction writing, journalism, or creative entrepreneurship. For SPs, satisfying work often involves opportunities to respond to concrete challenges. SFPs may enjoy working as nurses, therapists, or caregivers, while STPs may become athletes, first responders, mechanics, surgeons, etc.

Learning & Teaching Styles

J types are often said to be more formal or traditional in their methods and preferences than P types. This is clearly the case when it comes to teaching and learning.

Js are typically at home with "traditional" modes of education. They believe in the time-honored roles of teacher and pupil. They also tend to gravitate toward conventional career paths, including seeking formal endorsements, such as college degrees and professional licenses. Obtaining a degree or license grants them the sense of confidence and legitimacy they desire before moving forward in their work.

P types, by contrast, are more skeptical toward traditional educational methods and more open to unconventional alternatives. This is due, at least in part, to their desire for self-directed learning. Just as they like to make their own laws, they also like to be in charge of what and how they learn. Ps can also be more tepid about degrees and licensing, feeling that the most talented or qualified people are not necessarily the ones with degrees. ITPs, in particular, may feel they can "make something of themselves" from the ground up, obviating the need to obtain a degree simply to placate prospective employers.

Js are also naturally inclined to teach, advise, and instruct others. What is interesting about J teachers is, because their introverted judging function (Ti or Fi) comes after their extraverted judging function (Te or Fe) in their functional stack, they may not have personally mastered whatever they happen to be teaching (especially if involving a practical skill). In other words, they may be better at teaching and correcting others than teaching or improving themselves. While often making excellent teachers, their slowness in applying their own advice may at times earn them unwanted recognition as hypocrites (especially EJs).

Ps are the opposite. They are naturally better at teaching themselves than teaching others. Since their first judging function (Ti or Fi) is introverted, they are wired to personally trial information before distributing it outwardly. Hence, if they are going to teach at all, they often prefer to do so by example. P athletes, for instance, may simply advise their understudies to "watch and learn." Ps may also teach by facilitation. Instead of lecturing (a favored method among Js), P facilitators ask questions and encourage students to personally explore and experiment with a topic, encouraging self-guided learning. Montessori schooling is a great example of a P approach to teaching and learning, honoring and promoting individuality in the learning process.

To further illustrate these J-P differences, consider this example. An INTJ friend and I often talk about online marketing strategies. He enjoys reading about the latest and greatest techniques, then proceeds to advise me how I should move forward. He has said on more than one occasion, "I would much rather teach these things than implement them myself." As a self-directed INTP, there is never a time when I automatically implement his advice. I do, however, take it into consideration. And unlike my friend, my first preference is never to teach others, but to explore and experiment with things to see what works for me.

Closing Remarks

As may be evident from the extensiveness and particularity of the above discussion, the J-P dimension has long comprised one of my primary interest areas. Over the past decade, I've intermittently worked to refine my understanding of its many nuances and complexities. At one point, I was ready to give up on typology because I saw the J-P dimension as fraught with problems and inconsistencies. Fortunately, I was able to hang on long enough to reconcile what I initially saw as perplexing or contradictory. I am now convinced of its conceptual and empirical veracity and feel fortunate to share my discoveries with you. And while we have covered many of the foremost J-P themes in this chapter, there remains more for us to explore and review in Chapter 16.

Summary

Characteristics of J Types:

- Outwardly firm, direct, and opinionated
- Undeterred from directly expressing their views or wishes (especially EJs); utilize declarative statements
- Tone and mannerisms convey a sense of closure, seriousness, or formalness
- Others may turn to them for answers or decision-making
- See planning as a way of reducing risk and ensuring desirable outcomes
- Experience and express convergence in beliefs / worldview
- More apt to prefer structure and predictability in work settings
- Prefer "traditional" methods of teaching and learning, such as lectures or direct instruction
- Not necessarily neat, tidy, organized, uptight, or punctual
- Less restless and less dependent on a breadth of activities for stimulation (especially IJs)

Characteristics of P Types:

- Outwardly open, receptive, and adaptable
- Can be reluctant to state things directly (especially IPs); may express themselves in a more tangential fashion (e.g., using hints or questions)

- Are typically unenthusiastic about making detailed plans, especially when involving other people; enjoy the uncertainty of leaving things open-ended
- Slow to reach closure in beliefs or decisions
- Often viewed as good, non-judgmental listeners
- Can be skeptical toward external laws; prefer to make and follow their own rules
- Desire variety, novelty, informality, and minimal structure at work
- Often prefer to teach themselves (especially IPs); teach others by example or facilitation
- Not necessarily messy, disorganized, procrastinating, or chronically late
- Often restless, turning to a breadth of activities for stimulation (especially EPs)

Common J-P Mistypings

Perhaps more than any other personality dimension, mistypings abound in the J-P domain. For reasons we've touched on in this and earlier chapters, J-P mistypings are particularly common among introverts. Among the most frequent is IFPs misidentifying as IFJs. This may stem from IFPs' status as inner judgers (Fi), as well as over-identification with their inferior Te. They therefore come to see themselves as responsible, dutiful, and organized, traits they associate with the J preference. INFPs may also mistake their Fi-Ne combination for Ni, mistaking deep feeling (Fi) combined with broad intuition (Ne) for deep intuition (Ni).

Of all types, EJs seem least likely to error in their J-P classification, as EJs are in many ways the purest embodiment of judging. And while most EPs correctly identify their J-P preference, those who are more assertive and forceful via their tertiary function (Fe or Te) may be prone to mistype as judgers.

Other mistypings involve over-focusing on a given element of the J-P dimension. For instance, most ESFPs have a strong concern and eye for aesthetics. In striving to maintain the appearance of things, they are naturally inclined toward tidiness. Their tertiary Te function may also contribute an interest in organizing. So if an ESFP were to over-emphasize the issue of external order, it is easy to see how they might mistype as ESFJs.

Part III

CLARIFYING YOUR FUNCTIONS

Chapter 7

INTRODUCTION TO
THE EIGHT FUNCTIONS

Having now explored the eight preferences, you probably have at least a ballpark idea of your personality type. And while the preferences can be helpful for determining your personality type and gaining a basic understanding of the ingredients of type, they do not give us the whole story. To obtain a deeper level of understanding and get "more bang for our typological buck," studying the functions is a must.

Broadly speaking, the functions can be conceived as universal tools of mind. Even in other animals, we see evidence of emotion (F), pragmatic logic (T), instinct / intuition (N), and sensation (S). Over the course of history and evolution, we see increased differentiation of these tools, including the eventual emergence of the eight functions and the sixteen personality types.

In this and upcoming chapters, we will explore Jung's eight psychological functions, helping you further clarify and understand your personality type.

Introverted vs. Extraverted Functions

In this book's Introduction, we touched on the how the four basic functions (S, N, T, and F) can take on introverted and extraverted forms. And while the S, N, T, and F functions retain some of their basic properties, their E-I direction does modify them in significant ways. These modifications are to some extent predictable based on what we know about introversion and extraversion, involving a sort of blending of introversion or extraversion with the inherent nature of the function. Extraverted Intuition (Ne), for instance, represents a blending of the characteristics of extraversion with those of intuition. Because of the E-I influence, all the extraverted functions will display certain similarities, with the same being true for the introverted functions.

Like extraverts, the extraverted functions are concerned with external phenomena:

- Se with novel, outer sensations and experiences, as well as keeping up appearances
- Ne with perceiving and recombining circulating ideas, theories, and possibilities
- Fe with establishing interpersonal rapport, meeting others' needs, and observing social norms
- Te with analyzing and optimizing external systems, methods, and operations

Like introverts, the introverted functions are concerned with internal phenomena:

- Si with the remembered past and inner sensations
- Ni with insights and impressions from the subconscious mind
- Fi with personal feelings, tastes, and morals
- Ti with subjective logic, methods, and strategies

Just as extraverts are outgoing and expansive in their affairs, the extraverted functions are characteristically broad, extensive, and expansive in their workings:

- Se broadly surveys sensations and experiences.
- Ne extensively explores and multiplies ideas, patterns, and possibilities.
- Fe works to establish broad social networks and consensus of values and feelings.
- Te multiplies facts, rules, policies, and definitions.

Just as introverts are apt to display a narrower bandwidth of activities and interests, the introverted functions are narrower in scope and more intensive in their focus. They tend to reduce, consolidate, or restrict rather than expand and multiply:

- Si intensively draws on a limited set of perspectives, behaviors, traditions, and conventions.
- Ni penetrates deeply to identify underlying motives and causes; its theories are convergent.
- Fi deeply explores and refines personal tastes and feelings; it may also emotionally invest in a select few individuals or causes.
- Ti uses deep logic to formulate and refine subjective methods and strategies; it also takes a reductive approach toward knowledge.

Judging vs. Perceiving Functions

We can also make predictions about the functions based on their status as judging or perceiving functions. As we've seen, the judging functions (T and F) are charged with making evaluations and decisions that furnish a sense of order, direction, control, and predictability. The perceiving functions (S and N) are concerned with absorbing, extracting, retaining, or synthesizing information. They help us enjoy and learn about internal and external phenomena.

In combination with an E-I direction, we can understand the judging functions as follows:

- Te seeks to impose rational order on external systems; it is outwardly controlling.
- Ti imposes rational order on the self and its objectives; it is concerned with self-regulation, self-direction, and self-control.
- Fe facilitates order and gives direction in the world of human relations; it seeks social and moral order.
- Fi is concerned with emotional and moral order of the self; like Ti, it is self-regulating and self-controlling.

When the perceiving functions take on an E or I direction, we arrive at the following formulations:

- Se surveys a breadth of external sensations and experiences; it is characteristically open-ended and non-discriminating.
- Si retains, condenses, and recollects past information; it also perceives inner bodily sensations.
- Ne surveys and recombines a breadth of ideas and possibilities; like Se, it is characteristically open-ended and non-discriminating.
- Ni collects and synthesizes information to produce convergent impressions, insights, answers, and theories.

Overview of the Eight Functions

While we will soon explore the functions in greater depth, for the sake of convenience and reference, I've summarized what we've learned about functions thus far, providing a quick overview of each. For the extraverted functions, I've added observations of how they present outwardly (the introverted functions are not readily observed from without).

Introverted Intuition (Ni) collects conscious and subconscious information, and then synthesizes it to produce convergent impressions, insights, answers, and theories. It sees deep causes, patterns, and laws underlying sense data. It is characteristically penetrating and insightful.

Extraverted Intuition (Ne) surveys and creatively recombines a breadth of ideas, associations, patterns, and possibilities. It is characteristically innovative, divergent, open-ended, and non-discriminating. Outwardly, Ne users may present as scattered, random, quirky, witty, and ideationally curious.

Introverted Sensing (Si) retains, consolidates, and recollects historical and autobiographical information. It attends to and draws on a concentrated body of past experiences, routines, and traditions (i.e., the "tried and true"). It forgoes the constant pursuit of new or broad experiences, finding safety and security in stability and consistency. It also surveys inner bodily sensations.

Extraverted Sensing (Se) seeks extensive outer stimulation in the "here and now"—new sights, sounds, tastes, experiences, etc. It is open-ended and non-discriminating with respect to new experiences. It can also be associated with image-consciousness and observation skills, displaying a keen eye for detail. Outwardly, it may manifest as a recurrent desire for activities beyond talking ("Let's do something!").

Introverted Thinking (Ti) utilizes deep and nuanced logic to examine techniques, problems, concepts, or theories. It seeks self-regulation and self-optimization through the development of personal skills, methods, and strategies. It takes a skeptical and reductive approach toward knowledge.

Extraverted Thinking (Te) uses explicit logic, including standardized methods, measurements, policies, and procedures, to make systems and operations more rational, efficient, or effective. This often involves working as part of an institution, be it corporate, scientific, academic, etc. Outwardly, Te delivers opinions and directives in a firm, direct, measured, and unemotional fashion. It may at times be perceived as harsh, tactless, or unsympathetic.

Introverted Feeling (Fi) explores and refines personal tastes and feelings, contributing to a strong sense of personal uniqueness. It is self-regulating and self-controlling, working to maintain inner emotional and moral order. It may also emotionally invest in a limited number of love objects, be they persons, animals, hobbies, or causes.

Extraverted Feeling (Fe) surveys a breadth of human emotions, values, and morals. It strives toward interpersonal rapport, consensus, and continuity. It can also be associated with effective communication and social intelligence, facilitating growth and transformation in others. Outwardly, it delivers opinions and directives in a direct yet tactful way, often with a sense of emotional urgency and conviction.

Chapter 8

INTRODUCTED
INTUITION (NI)

Primary roles: To collect conscious and subconscious information, then synthesize it to produce impressions, insights, answers, and theories; to see deep causes, patterns, and laws underlying sense data

Most prominent in: INTJs & INFJs; also prominent in ENTJs & ENFJs

Associated with: Deep perceptiveness and insight, deep "knowing," theoretical genius, powers of analysis and focus, advising and troubleshooting

Famous INJs: Plato, Jesus, Nietzsche, Jung, Steven Hawking

Ni serves as the dominant function for INFJs and INTJs, as well as the auxiliary for ENFJs and ENTJs. It is by far the rarest of all functions, making NJs the rarest of all types. According to the *MBTI Manual*, there are only about half the number of NJs as NPs. Therefore, from a purely statistical standpoint, individuals unsure of their status as an NJ versus an NP are far more likely to be NPs.

Although INJs are classified as J types, their dominant orientation is one of inner perceiving (Ni). Ni synthesizes and delivers information from the subconscious mind. INJs often receive brilliant insights that seem to come "from nowhere." Ni can therefore seem to have a magical character, one that is envied by other types. However magical or supernatural its working may appear, Ni can be understood on a more rational basis through the lens of typology.

First, it is important to understand that INJs' inferior function (Se) subconsciously gathers copious amounts of sensory information from the outside world. It then synthesizes and interprets this data, along with extant subconscious information, like assembling pieces of a puzzle. The end result, "the finished puzzle," comes in the form of an impression, theory, insight, or vision. Hence, what the ancients conceived as "revelations from God" may be better understood as the creative work of Ni and the subconscious mind. What is most remarkable and least understood is exactly how Ni manages to assemble these puzzles so quickly and effectively.

Drawing on their powers of Ni, INJs excel when it comes to assessing the entirety of a situation and quickly "reading" what is happening. Like the prophets of old, they may get a strong sense of how things might unfold if they were to continue along their current trajectory. While not going so far as to consider INJ psychics, we might say they are skilled at seeing the "dark skies before the storm."

When expressed a la their auxiliary Fe or Te, INJ impressions are often rather critical in nature. INFJs, in particular, can seem rather negative and intense in their pronouncements. To other types, they may seem to routinely "make mountains out of molehills." In most cases, however, other types are less attuned to the signs of the brewing storm. They may deny that a problem even exists until they find themselves stuck in a torrential downpour.

An INFJ recently confessed to me that she constantly feels out of sync with the world. When she feels panicked, others are calm. And by the time others are panicked—when the storm hits—she has become calm. It's almost as though once INJs have delivered their critique or warning, they feel they have done all they can do and the issue is out of their hands.

The Visual Nature of Ni

It is often said that human beings rely more heavily on vision than we do our other senses. This seems especially true of INJs, who often ascribe a strong (inner) visual element to their Ni. INJs often think by way of images rather than words. Their intuitions may manifest as symbols, images, dreams, or patterns. The visual nature of Ni might also tie into their Se inferior, which is also a highly visual function.

Considering the visual nature of Ni and Se, it is no surprise that many INJs are sensitive to beauty—visual, metaphorical, or otherwise. The INJ philosopher Jean Paul Sartre once confessed: "I'm only a desire for beauty." Another INJ, Friedrich Nietzsche, famously proclaimed that "Life is only valuable as an aesthetic phenomenon." This penchant for beauty helps explain why so many INJs enjoy creating or appreciating art. Many also prefer visual representations of information, be it through pictures, charts, diagrams, etc.

Visual processing also seems advantageous for reconciling paradoxical opposites—a signature strength of Ni. In order to label or otherwise describe something in words, it must be extracted and demarcated from its surrounding context. While undoubtedly useful, this requires keeping things separate and distinct, which can make it difficult to solve problems involving competing or contradicting ideas. To the rational mind, two contradictory assertions cannot simultaneously coexist—one of the them must be rendered false. But according to Jung, the unconscious mind, through its innate creativity, is adept at reconciling opposites and transcending paradoxes. The beauty of visual processing is that it doesn't have the same rules or impediments as verbal processing. So problems that seem intractable to linear or logical solutions may at times be resolved by way of images or symbols. Indeed, one reason INJs often make formidable theorists is they can approach problems in non-linear or non-verbal ways, allowing them to consider multiple perspectives simultaneously. In short, intuition can at times solve problems that logic or verbal processing cannot because it is not bound by the same set of rules or methods.

An INFJ friend of mine is a champion of paradoxical or Janusian thinking. In our discussions of philosophy, she has repeatedly sought to transcend traditional categorizations and dichotomies by claiming that reality is at once relative and absolute, subjective and objective, temporal and eternal, etc. Again, to the rational mind, which is bound by such dichotomies, such notions can be difficult to comprehend, much less accept. From the perspective of Ni, however, there is a sense that all things can be reconciled through the special lens of intuition.

Symbols and symbolism also tie into the visual nature of Ni and Se. INJs often report a deep sense of meaning and wholeness when engaging with symbols. Integrating idea (N) and image (S), mental (N) and physical (S), potential (N) and actual (S), symbols are one way INJs (and ENPs) attempt to marry their dominant and inferior functions. Jung was convinced that engagement with symbols, whether through dream analysis or other means, was integral to psychospiritual growth and well-being. This should not surprise us, of course, since Jung himself was likely an INJ.

Deep Knowing

While technically not a judging function, Ni works convergently, providing singular answers and solutions to complex problems. INJs commonly report that solutions come to them in a flash of insight— an "aha!" moment. This may occur while dreaming or awake, but often comes suddenly and all at once. Nietzsche, most certainly an INJ, described his intuitive process in the following way:

> "Something profoundly convulsive…suddenly becomes visible and audible with indescribable definiteness and exactness… There is an ecstasy whose terrific tension is sometimes released by a flood of tears…There is a feeling that one is utterly out of hand…Everything occurs without volition, as if an eruption of freedom, independence, power, and divinity. The spontaneity of the images and similes is most remarkable; one loses all perception of what is imagery and simile; everything offers itself as the most immediate, exact, and simple means of expression."

While Nietzsche was no stranger to hyperbole, it is clear that Ni insights can break into consciousness in a powerful and convincing fashion. This is why Ni is often associated with a deep sense of conviction and certainty. Indeed, for INJs, *believing* something is not at all the same thing as *knowing* something. INJs typically feel they *know*, on a deep intuitive level, that their insights are true. They differ from ENPs in this respect, who often fail to experience the same degree of confidence and conviction toward their intuitions. In most cases, ENPs respond to their intuitions with excitement or enthusiasm rather than a deep sense of conviction or knowing.

Once INJs have received an Ni insight, they must work to flesh it out. This involves articulating or illustrating it in a way that others can understand. This is where their auxiliary function (Fe or Te) enters the picture. Its role is to unpack the intuition, sort of like decompressing a computer file. This process can at times be difficult and painstaking. It may even take longer than birthing the intuition itself. But in order for others to understand and get behind their intuitions, INJs must do their best to translate them. For INTJs, this might entail producing a technical framework or formula, while INFJs might turn to analogies, illustrations, or metaphors.

Deep Perception

INJs perceive things quite differently than other types. They don't focus on or give credence to surface appearances in the way that ESPs might. Rather, their focus is more penetrating, diving deep to uncover hidden causes, motives, and essences. We might liken Ni to a deep-sea diver. While most people enjoy swimming or snorkeling near the surface of the water, Ni seeks to dive as deeply as possible, apprehending an entirely different world than what is visible from the surface.

In gaining knowledge and insight into deeper phenomena, INJs naturally want to enlighten others about their insights. Part of this involves correcting others' faulty perceptions about people or the world. INJs see inaccurate perceptions as dangerous and destructive, as bad perceptions can only beget bad ideas and bad actions. This is why INJs place such high value on truth. They are resolute in believing that truth can be revealed through their Ni and that others should therefore be open to hearing and heeding it. They can get discouraged and frustrated, however, when others fail to understand or respond to their insights with a similar sense of gravity or conviction.

Deep Theories, Timeless Truths

Part of deep perception is apprehending *deep* or *timeless* truths. Considering the ideas of INJs such as Plato, Jesus, Jung, or Stephen Hawking, for instance, we get a sense of the profundity and timelessness of Ni theories. Plato is well-known for his "eternal Forms," Jesus for his doctrine of "eternal life," Jung for his theories on personality types, archetypes, and the collective unconscious (all of which are independent of time), and Hawking for his work on the timeless laws of physics. One reason these ideas have withstood the test of time is Ni has a way of "getting to the bottom of things," of capturing unchanging essences and universal truths.

Because of Ni's knack for navigating metaphysical and other timeless ideas, INJ theorists are typically more interested in developing deep, universal theories than small-scale, historically-contingent ones. ENPs, by contrast, who use Ne as their dominant function, tend to exhibit stronger interests in local or historically-contingent phenomena. This is because Ne works transcontextually, along a horizontal axis, and may fail to grasp or take interest in deeper laws and essences.

For example, ENFP film critics will often focus on a film's unique and particular qualities—its cast, authorship, cultural and historical influences, etc. They are apt to evaluate the film on its own terms and according to its own context, viewing it as a unique creation on the stage of history. They may also compare it to other films that Ne brings to mind. INFJ critics, by contrast, might be less intrigued by a film's particulars, at least from a theoretical standpoint. While its unique features may certainly be interesting from an entertainment perspective, they are of less theoretical interest to Ni. For Ni, a film's particulars are mere iterations of deeper human patterns (this relates to our Chapter 4 discussion of the Ni essence of a table). INFJ critics might therefore be inclined to highlight the way in which various eternal archetypes manifested in the film or how its depictions of good and evil represent projections of the moral struggles of the human psyche.

From this, we can see how the INJ's deep focus has a way of stripping away local and historical factors in order to highlight perennial patterns. And while ENPs may also be aware of deep patterns such as archetypes, archetypes are likely to play a smaller or more tangential role in their thinking. For ENPs, an ongoing stream of new theories and ideas is typically more interesting than dwelling on something as static as eternal archetypes.

Ni & the Brain

In his book, *The Neuroscience of Personality*, UCLA personality researcher, Dr. Dario Nardi, explores the neuroscientific basis for the functions. Nardi describes the Ni brain state as "zen-like," a state of relaxed awareness that straddles the conscious and unconscious mind. Unlike the Ne mind, which is characteristically restless and hyperactive, the Ni mind is more calm and synchronized. While other types may experience something similar when they are "in the zone," the state of relaxed awareness is more of the default for INJs. According to Nardi (an INJ himself), it's as though Ni uses the whole brain to "realize" answers.

But this doesn't tell the whole story. There seem to be at least two distinguishable modes of Ni. The first is the calm, relaxed, and zen-like state we just discussed. We might call it the *incubation stage*. The other mode, which we might call the *hatching stage*, occurs when intuitions have completely formed and are breaking into full consciousness. This stage is more focused and intense, such as in our earlier quotation of Nietzsche. During the hatching stage, the INJ is in an even deeper state of trance and focus. One INJ has likened it to peering into a narrow tunnel and sensing that there is no limit to the level of depth one can obtain. In such moments, the outside world falls away and there is a sense of full immersion in the intuition.

The "whole-brained" way in which INJs process information may partly explain the cogency of their theories and insights, as well as their sense of conviction about their intuitions. In essence, we might describe an Ni "moment of knowing" as having the entire brain "on the same page" or "the same wavelength." As we will see in the next chapter, Ne manifests quite differently, involving random, asynchronous patterns of brain activity.

Ni & the Eyes

Though not addressed by Nardi, eye movements may serve as additional empirical clues for determining when a particular function is being used. Generally speaking, the extraverted functions are thought to be associated with a direct forward gaze (Fe, Te) or side-to-side darting movements (Se and especially Ne). The introverted functions appear to be associated with a downward (and potentially upward) gaze, suggesting the attention is turned inwardly. This make sense from a spatial perspective if we think of extraverted perception as being broad (i.e., horizontal axis) and the introverted functions as being deep and inward (i.e., vertical axis).

More specifically, when Ni is being intensively used, the eyelids drop to half-mast as the gaze orients downward and converges, as if looking into a narrow tunnel. This gaze is consistent with the focused and synchronized nature of the Ni brain state, which seeks to zero-in on an answer. To my knowledge, this hasn't been confirmed with careful empirical studies. Nevertheless, some typologists believe the eyes can clue us into which functions are being employed.

There may also be a relationship between Ni and nearsightedness. After all, if the Ni user's eyes are frequently fixing on a nearby point, opening the door to "in-sight," then distant sights (i.e., extraverted perceptions) could feasibly be neglected or deprioritized. Conversely, we might predict EPs to be disposed to farsightedness, since their eyes are constantly scanning outwardly. EJs and IPs, whose dominant function is a *judging* function, may fail to display any consistent pattern in this regard, since the eyes are primarily organs of *perception*. As we saw with eye movements, these predictions, to my knowledge, have not been carefully studied. I mention them because they are theoretically interesting and may provide further clues for deciphering one's type.

Chapter 9

EXTRAVERTED INTUITION (NE)

Primary Role: To broadly explore, synthesize, and express ideas, associations, and possibilities

Most prominent In: ENTPs & ENFPs; also prominent in INTPs & INFPs

Associated With: Brainstorming, innovative / artistic / ideational creativity, divergent thinking, holistic / weblike associations, a nose for promising new enterprises

Famous ENPs: Benjamin Franklin, Walt Disney, Steve Jobs, Ellen DeGeneres, Jon Stewart, John Edward

ENPs use Extraverted Intuition (Ne) as their dominant function, while INPs wield it as their auxiliary function. Ne is more divergent and expansive than its introverted cousin, Ni. NPs feel compelled to explore *all* the options and possibilities ("the possibilities are endless!"), making it difficult for them to draw conclusions or make decisions. Moreover, as an extraverted function, the nature and workings of Ne are more accessible to outsiders. NPs often present as open-minded, receptive, creative, inquisitive, random, distractible, and playful. They love playing with words, ideas, associations, and quips. Ne quickly sees connections and associations that other types may not, contributing much in the way of wit, cleverness, and ingenuity.

Because of the rather chaotic and random nature of Ne, some NPs may struggle with verbal fluency or ideational cogency. Their speech can be sporadic and their ideas incoherent as they haphazardly bounce from one idea to the next. I have often described the verbal expression of Ne as "brainstorming aloud." It's as if the Ne brain is so flooded with intercoursing ideas that it struggles to funnel them into a linear, streamlined format. This can at times render interlocutors lost and confused, unsure of what the hyper-minded NP is trying to say.

A primary function of Ne is scanning for relationships or patterns within pools of ideas. This may occur at any time or place, but is often stimulated by activities like reading, writing, conversing, travelling, watching movies, listening to music, etc. With each new Ne association comes a sense of pleasure, and sometimes even excitement. While NPs naturally assume that everything is connected in some fashion, they love spinning new strands to add to their existing web of Ne connections.

The notion that everything is connected can give Ne a sort of mystical flavor. It engenders a sense of anticipation for what God or the universe might have in store at any given moment. Jung's notion of *synchronicity*, roughly defined as the experience of a meaningful coincidence or connection, is common among NP types. ENPs, for whom Ne is dominant, seem particularly attuned to "signs" and synchronicities perceived to bring meaning and direction to their life. Since their N (which we might roughly associate with the metaphysical) is extraverted, many NPs are open to the idea of an exterior spiritual realm. Religion, astrology, spirits, psychic capacities, and all varieties of psi phenomena can be intriguing to Ne types, especially ENPs. Since Ni is introverted, INJs can be less confident about, or intrigued by, the notion of external spiritual phenomena.

Indeed, because Ne is so open and non-discriminating, NPs may struggle to rule anything out with certainty. For Ne, anything is within the realm of possibility. Even when NPs' Ti or Fi pushes for conclusions, Ne rallies for further exploration. Ne's drive for open-ended exploration leads NPs to entertain a breadth of perspectives. They can see truth on both sides of an issue without forming premature conclusions. They may even find themselves convinced by one argument, only to feel similarly entranced by its counterpoint.

While open-mindedness is undoubtedly a signature strength of Ne, it can sometimes hamper productivity and follow-through. Leaning too heavily on Ne can seduce NPs into chasing rabbit trails that derail their attempts at focused work. Ne openness can also make NPs uncomfortable around types (typically J types) whose assertions seem too firm, conclusive, or unnuanced.

Skepticism is a close companion to Ne openness. In the same way NPs struggle to deem anything false, they can be slow to endorse something as true; both are characteristics of a truly open mind. Ne can quickly envision alternatives to nearly anything stated as fact. Making matters worse, NPs are sensitive to anomalies and outliers, even to the point of discounting (sometimes prematurely) an entire theory on account of a single inconsistency.

Despite their sensitivity to "holes" or inconsistencies in others' theories, NPs may not always apply the same skepticism to their own ideas, at least not initially. When NPs feel excited about a new connection or idea, they are inclined to happily ride their Ne train of thought wherever it leads. It may take a few days, after their initial enthusiasm has waned, for them to step back and consider alternative explanations. In short, NPs are a curious admixture of openness and skepticism. They can be enthusiasts one moment, skeptics the next. This can make life with an NP a challenging affair, since their beliefs and passions can seem ever-fluctuating.

Ne can also be associated with restlessness. NPs may find themselves longing to escape certain situations or circumstances to experience more freedom, novelty, or autonomy. They may be inspired to quit their job, break off a relationship, or ditch a party in hopes of discovering something more interesting. NPs who consistently act on such promptings may be viewed as fickle, erratic, or irresponsible.

Doubting & Dithering

NPs are hardwired to second-guess themselves. They may feel wholly confident about an idea one day, only to feel ambivalent toward it the next. They find it difficult not to see things as grey or ambiguous. Ne can have a destabilizing effect on NPs' psyche, invoking them to seek more information *ad infinitum*. If NPs consistently acquiesce to such promptings, they can end up feeling lost and aimless. At times, they may feel overwhelmed, even paralyzed, by a deluge of Ne options.

Considering the non-committal ways of Ne, NPs can flounder when it comes to making big decisions, such as choosing a college major, marital partner, or career path. They may find themselves wishing that external circumstances could somehow decide for them, that fate might step in and provide direction. They may turn to religion, astrology, psychics, or other sorts of external signposts. In some cases, they may, wittingly or not, even aid the hands of fate. If wanting out of a bad relationship, for instance, they may fail to conjure the courage or conviction required to directly confront their partner. So instead, they may passively or subconsciously go about sabotaging the relationship, hoping that, in the end, their partner will do the dirty work for them.

Dithering NPs may also turn to others, especially to J types, for their guidance and counsel. Unfortunately, this often fails to resolve the issue, since Ne keeps pushing for additional perspectives and information. In some cases, seeking more information merely delays the inevitable or further clouds the essential issue.

While NPs may yearn for more certainty in their lives, absolute certainty is more of an ideal than a reality for these types. It's as though the order-seeking left brain will be forever incapable of keeping pace with their chaos-inducing right brain. And while making decisions or drawing conclusions may feel like a perpetual thorn in NPs' side, it is helpful to remember that whatever Ne lacks in decisiveness is more than made up for in openness and creativity.

Ne vs. Ni

NPs and NJs both display certain qualities associated with intuition generally, such as a concern for the ideational, theoretical, and metaphysical. Despite these similarities, Ne and Ni also differ in some important ways.

Ni interprets narrowly from great breadth (Se), equipping INJs to sure-handedly procure convergent theories, answers, and insights. Ne, by contrast, interprets broadly from great depth, drawing from an intensive storehouse of inner experience (Si). In consulting Si's deep knowledge of what has been, Ne puts forth a breadth of possible *"what could be's."* Unlike Ni, Ne feels there is too much ground to cover to explore any single topic in great depth.

As an extraverted function, Ne is also more reliant on circulating ideas than Ni is. NPs turn to extant theories and ideas to make new associations and to stimulate their creative process. INJs, by contrast, are less reliant on circulating ideas, turning inward for answers and insights (Ni). NPs can therefore be seen as more dependent on the outside world for their N processing than INJs are. This difference is evident when comparing ENP and INJ intellectuals. Namely, ENPs seem more concerned with knowing which thinkers and theories are in vogue. They are also notorious for "name dropping," constantly referencing various books or theorists to support their arguments.

Webs (Ne) & Hierarchies (Ni)

Ne and Ni also differ in how they perceive and handle information. The Ne approach can be envisioned as holistic, horizontal, or weblike. When it comes to the issue of health, for instance, NPs gravitate toward various "holistic" perspectives that view health as a sort of crossroads of mind, body, and spirit.

To illustrate, imagine the concept of health centered in a web of related concepts. If each of these concepts was placed in its own circle, we would see a number of different concepts overlapping with the concept of health. It is through these sorts of horizontal associations and overlaps that Ne goes about understanding the world.

NPs also rely heavily on contrasts and comparisons, a method I employ routinely throughout this book. Instead of simply defining the personality functions on their own terms, I frequently compare and contrast them with related functions. For NPs, contrasts and comparisons are preferred to explicit definitions. NPs trust the process of emergent understanding, sensing that the mind will make the appropriate connections and "read between the lines." This all relates to a process called "holistic spiraling," which Ben Kovitz nicely describes as follows:

> "One makes a contrast or comparison to establish reference for a term, then uses that term to state a proposition. That proposition is then contrasted or compared with other propositions...In contrast to rhetoric guided by Te, the conclusion cannot be stated at the beginning. Nearly all of the rhetoric is concerned primarily with establishing a shared understanding of reference points in reality, in terms of which the conclusion will be framed. The rhetoric of Te more typically begins with a conclusion framed in terms of an already shared conceptual framework, followed by reasons to establish that conclusion..."

For Ne, conclusions cannot be stated at the outset, but are anticipated to emerge organically over time. In this sense, Ne resembles what are commonly known as "bottom-up" or "grassroots" approaches. In bottom-up systems, such as a pure democracy, the outcome of a vote is never known at the outset. New laws or policies are the result, not the starting point, of the process. We see a similar process at work in NP writers. Part of my own writing process, for instance, involves blindly following the flow of Ne consciousness wherever it leads. I hardly ever know exactly where my writing is heading, and I often find myself surprised by the new associations and directions that emerge over time. Hence, my early drafts can be rather chaotic and disjointed.

Ni can be viewed as more linear, vertical, or hierarchical in its approach (this is partly why NJs are often viewed as more "left-brained" than NPs). It penetrates deep rather than wide, seeing things in terms of structured hierarchies rather than webs (especially when paired with Te). NTJs, in particular, prefer clear and explicit definitions and structure. As we saw in the quote by Kovitz, their rhetoric often commences with a set of definitions or conclusions. Unsurprisingly, this is exactly what we see in "top-down" approaches. One can observe this, for instance, in companies where executives make decisions and issue directives, while those lower in the hierarchy are expected to carry out those orders. The organization of a text book—replete with headings, subheadings, definitions, and so on—is another example of top-down, hierarchical structuring.

Like NPs, NJ writers also tap into a stream of N consciousness. The difference between the Ne and Ni writing process is largely one of foresight and structure. Namely, NJs seem to have a clearer upfront sense of where they are headed with their writing. Similar to what we saw with Ni intuitions, there is a sense of *knowing* that permeates the NJ writing process. In some respects, NJs may feel they are merely transcribing what they already know, while NPs feel they are exploring and discovering surprising new connections at every turn. It's like the difference between describing and analyzing what one already sees versus creatively piecing something together from scratch. The Ne process seems more "blind" than that of Ni (this relates to the maze metaphor used to describe P types in Chapter 6).

Because of the more convergent nature of Ni, NJs' writing also tends to be more naturally structured, constrained, and streamlined. They have fewer possibilities to contend with than the divergent minds of NPs. This makes NJs well-suited for certain types of academic, scientific, technical, or non-fiction writing, while NPs often feel more at home with poetry, fiction, or more open-ended varieties of non-fiction.

In light of the above differences, NJs and NPs may fail to see eye-to-eye with regard to both the content and structuring of information. More specifically, NJs can be dismissive of what they see as the "superficial" associations of Ne, as well as the holistic (or what NJs might consider "arbitrary" or "chaotic") nature of Ne rhetoric. Returning to our earlier example, NJs will generally agree that health is influenced by a breadth of factors. However, they typically see Ne conceptions of "holistic health" as hopelessly vague and not particularly helpful. Toward the end of greater specificity and operational usefulness, NJs prefer to approach the mind and body as two separate systems, which they feel should remain distinct with respect to both theory and practice. NJs are far less open to, or enthusiastic about, blurring or muddling the boundaries between disciplines (e.g., "interdisciplinary studies") than horizontally-minded NPs tend to be. Due to the narrower and more in-depth approach of Ni, NJs see disciplinary boundaries as essential to plumbing the depths of any subject area.

Art, Nature, & Lifestyle

NPs and NJs also differ in their lifestyle preferences, as well as in their attitudes toward art and nature. NPs, especially INFPs, are often well-described as "earthy" in both appearance and lifestyle. The hippy culture is emblematic of many of the attitudes and fashions of NP types. Female NPs tend to go lighter on make-up and are generally less concerned with looking "pretty" (Se) than they are with dressing creatively or idiosyncratically (Ne). Designer clothing, high-priced meals, or extravagant vacations are rarely high on their priority list.

Many NPs (especially INFPs) are lovers of nature, not to mention anything "natural" or "organic." They may take to trails, mountains, or the woods to "find themselves" or "reconnect with nature." Vegans and vegetarians are also commonplace among NPs, as are those drawn to mind-body practices like yoga and meditation. NPs are keen on exploring and invoking the natural or "spiritual" healing capacities of the mind and body. In the same vein, many are intrigued with Eastern philosophies and religions.

NPs commonly content themselves with rather meager or Bohemian living arrangements. Their living spaces are often adorned with an array of second-hand furniture and decor. Some NPs will join communes, try their luck with van living, or explore other alternative lifestyles. Such offbeat lifestyles appeal to their Si's propensity for material conservativism, as well as their Ne's penchant for creatively crafting makeshift solutions.

While some NPs may take interest in the fine arts, they are typically rather unpretentious about it. They make little distinction in value between "the arts" and more everyday sorts of crafts. This is likely due to the fact that, like SJs (who also use Ne-Si), one of NPs' chief artistic interests involves recombining (Ne) existing resources (Si). They even do this with their dress. Rather than constantly running out to buy new clothes (like ESPs might), they cleverly piece together "new" outfits from their existing wardrobe.

On the whole, NJs tend to be more traditional and conventional in both their appearance and lifestyle. While they (especially INFJs) may go through unconventional periods in which they feel compelled to express their uniqueness through bizarre fashions or fetishes, their need to do so is typically short-lived. NJs are less apt to pepper themselves with tattoos, experiment with drugs, or sample alternative lifestyles. In fact, many gravitate toward the opposite end of the spectrum, opting for a life of finery and sophistication (especially NFJs). Many NFJs relish fine food, clothing, and the arts (not the crafts!). They can therefore seem more pretentious than NP types, at least with respect to these sorts of S matters.

Ne-Ni Skepticism & Envy

NJs can be wary and skeptical of the ways and products of Ne. They may criticize NPs for their lack of ideational depth or cogency. Since Ne rambling tends to disrupt the more focused and streamlined workings of Ni, they may also feel frustrated or disoriented when engaging with a chatty NP type. In addition, they may see Ne methods as largely inefficient and ineffective, consuming far too much time and energy in formulating new ideas at every turn. NJs are apt to view their own Ni approach as far more efficacious, at least when it comes to producing convergent answers or insights.

With that said, there are also times when NJs may find themselves a bit jealous of NPs. They may envy NPs' ability to bring forth their N into the world in overt ways (i.e., to extravert N), such as through art, humor, innovation, and the like. Because Ne is extraverted, NPs tend to wear their N on their sleeves, readily showcasing their N talents. NJs may wish their powers of N (rather than their extraverted J function) could be revealed and esteemed as readily. They may also envy NPs' willingness to take risks and act in enterprising ways.

Similarly, NPs can have a love-hate relationship with Ni. They may criticize what they see as NJs' failure to acknowledge or appreciate the value of horizontal or weblike thinking. They may also see NJs as erecting unnecessary boundaries between knowledge areas, boundaries that prohibit the sorts of cross-contextual thinking that NPs relish. From the Ne perspective, Ni can seem overly narrow, rigid, or closed. NPs may therefore contend that NJs (as well as SJs) should be more open to alternative perspectives. In short, they criticize NJs for their lack of Ne.

At the same time, NPs can envy NJs' ability to perceive deeply. Rather than constantly bouncing from one topic to the next, NJs can incisively penetrate ever more deeply into a given topic or problem. NJs might fall into an extemporaneous, 30-minute lecture on a topic that NPs might have abandoned after 30 seconds. While there may be times when NPs are uninterested in entertaining NJ monologues, they can nonetheless appreciate NJs' capacity for going deep rather than wide. NPs may also covet the sense of conviction and certainty associated with Ni, wishing they too could experience a deep sense of "knowing."

Ne & the Brain

According to Dario Nardi, Ne is characterized by a "Christmas tree" brain-wave pattern. Unlike the more synchronized, zen-like state of Ni, the Christmas tree pattern is asynchronous, involving seemingly random activation of various brain regions. This random patterning is the neural correlate of NPs' propensity for horizontal and divergent modes of thought. When making creative or random associations, NPs are connecting information from diverse regions of the brain.

The active and sweeping nature of Ne may also be glimpsed in NPs' eye movements. When engaging their Ne, their eyes tend to dart broadly in a side-to-side fashion. Since the head often follows the path of the eyes, some NPs may also display frequent head turning. Whether moving the head, the eyes, or both, these movements can give the impression that NPs are searching for something in their surroundings. What they are actually seeking, however, is typically more abstract—new connections, patterns, words, ideas, possibilities, etc.

Chapter 10

INTROVERTED SENSING (SI)

Primary roles: To retain, condense, and recollect information; to consult past experiences, routines, and traditions; to perceive inner bodily sensations

Most prominent in: ISTJs & ISFJs; also prominent in ESTJs & ESFJs

Associated with: Routines, habits, valuing and preserving "the tried and true," material conservativism, high regard for traditions and authority

Famous ISJs: Dick Cheney, Martin Luther, Mother Theresa, George H.W. Bush

When thinking about sensing, we typically think in terms of the five senses. But the five senses really pertain more to Se than Si. While Se constantly seeks out new opportunities for stimulating the senses, Si is more interested in the routine and familiar. It is a careful and conservative function, drawing on existing resources, beliefs, or practices in lieu of exploring or developing new ones.

Most people are familiar with the notion of "learning through experience." This can be associated with Si, which guides and informs our behavior by consulting past experiences. To be sure, all types rely on memory and past experience to some extent, but for Si types (i.e., SJs) the past is granted higher priority and greater authority.

SJ clergy and news pundits, for instance, are constantly making arguments from history, viewing the past as the ultimate guide to, and authority for, present action. An Si minister may emphasize the deep importance of preserving and continuing in the traditions of the church, while SJ news pundits reference iconic individuals, documents, or periods of history (e.g., the "founding fathers," the Constitution, Lincoln, etc.) they feel should be emulated. Non-SJ types, by contrast, may wonder why we should grant the past such a high degree of authority. How, after all, are we to determine which historical authorities are to be followed and emulated? How do we know whether to believe the Bible or the Koran, Jesus or Mohammed? Is the decision merely arbitrary or should other evaluative criteria be admitted?

SJs are famous for embracing and defending "the tried and true." They are reluctant to change things they see as having a proven track record. "If it ain't broke, don't fix it!" is another Si mantra.

Growing attached to the routine, familiar, and expected, repetition seems to play a prominent role in Si. The more times SJs repeat something—eat a certain meal, listen to a specific song, etc.—the more likeable (or tolerable) it becomes. It was probably an SJ who, in noticing how his tastes shifted with repeated exposures, coined the phrase "it will grow on me." In many cases, if you can get an SJ to repeatedly try something, there's a decent chance they will eventually come to enjoy or at least better tolerate it.

In keeping with Si's appetite for consistency, SJs tend to fall into "daily routines," including routinized meal times and meal choices. My ISTJ mother is about as extreme as one can get in this respect. Despite having no history of food allergies or gastrointestinal problems, she dislikes most foods, including most fruits and vegetables. She eats nearly the same thing every day, even to the point of counting the number of tortilla chips that will flank her ham sandwich. When away from home, she typically lunchpails her meals, allowing her to continue to delight in her hopelessly bland and homogenous dietary regimen (I love you mom!).

Frugality is also commonplace among ISJs. Since Si is focused on conserving and making do with existing resources, ISJs naturally gravitate toward saving over spending. Of all types, they are the most likely to clip, organize, and redeem coupons, justifying their fastidiousness with phrases like "it all adds up." Relatedly, some ISJs may earn recognition as "hoarders," refusing to part ways with anything on account of its perceived sentimental or practical value.

SJs also take a conservative approach to their beliefs and worldview. As adults, they often persist in the beliefs, precepts, and traditions of their childhood. They are less disposed than other types to question the foundational tenets on which they were raised. However, as introverts, ISJs seem somewhat less inclined to function as frontline activists for their beliefs, preferring instead to spend time reflecting on the past and their cherished traditions. Many enjoy attending religious services or studying religious texts, activities that further reinforce their Si beliefs.

Dotting i's & Crossing t's

ISJs, in particular, take pride in "doing their duty," being obedient, and carrying out their responsibilities. Unlike other types, they are not opposed to receiving or following orders, especially from authorities they trust and respect. Many prefer work that involves following a set of pre-established rules, guidelines, or principles. They like order, structure, and predictability, all of which imbue their lives with a sense of safety and stability.

ISJs take their responsibilities seriously, down to the last detail. Indeed, their scrupulousness, or what some might pejoratively call "anal-retentiveness," may at times drive their non-SJ family members or co-workers crazy. In the workplace, ISJs may unwittingly irritate others with their tendency to ask litanies of questions to clarify exactly how things should be done. This can be frustrating to other types, especially P types, who prefer to leave things as vague and open as possible to preserve plenty of space for individual autonomy. So when ISJs keep pressing for more specifics and details, they may worry that this may lead to additional rules and policies that may further limit their freedom. Of course, P types need to understand that such ISJs are simply being themselves. Not only that, but every workplace needs ISJs to handle the routine and detailed tasks that no one else wants to do. ISJs make the most consistent and reliable employees. They work slowly and steadily until the job is done, meticulously attending to all the details along the way.

Outside the workplace, ISJs are far more easygoing than they are often given credit for. Since Si is a perceiving function, ISJs are actually drawn more to perceiving activities than controlling ones. Many ISJs enjoy engaging with children, playing word games, working crossword puzzles, crocheting or knitting, reading, singing, or playing an instrument. While ESJs may be a bit less scrupulous than ISJs, they tend to have more trouble relaxing and being leisurely.

Si & the "Inner Body"

Of all the functions, Te is decidedly the most "left-brained." It is logical, orderly, precise, and controlling. And while Si also entails certain left-brained features, such as attending to explicit rules, procedures, and details, it also has right-brained capacities that often go overlooked. Among these is the role of Si in attending to inner body sensations (e.g., pain, hunger, thirst, numbness, tingling, muscle tension), the body as felt and experienced from within.

When perceiving bodily sensations more globally, Si provides access to the simple yet sublime experience of embodiment, of "bodily being," apart from thought or outward stimuli. Historically, Eastern philosophical and religious traditions have done a far better job exploring and cultivating this sense of inner being than those of the West. Sensitivity to and awareness of bodily being can be developed through activities requiring close attention to one's inner body, such as yoga, Tai-Chi, Feldenkrais, meditation, various relaxation techniques, and so on. Masters of inner bodily awareness report a deep sense of bodily knowing and bodily wisdom. They learn what it means to trust and "listen to the body," allowing it to instinctively reveal the path to health and healing. In this sense, Si resembles the inner knowing of Ni, only that Si delivers physical insights and Ni metaphysical ones.

With that said, it seems that NPs (who also use Si) are more inclined to explore this dimension of Si than SJs are, at least in Western cultures. This may be due to the fact that, in the West, mind-body practices have yet to be fully embraced by mainstream culture. Consequently, SJs typically fail to receive the number of exposures required for these practices to "grow on them" and to thereby earn a place in their daily lives.

Si & Imagery

Another of Si's more right-brained capacities involves conjuring or recalling inner images. As with other types, some ISJs think more in images than they do in words. Those who think in terms of mechanical images (more commonly ISTJs) may be drawn to fields like science or engineering. Those who process images more holistically (more commonly ISFJs), such as envisioning faces or scenery, may show some measure of artistic interest or aptitude.

While individuals of any type may process information visually, SJs can be distinguished by their attention to past information. Many SJs, for instance, can impressively recall dates, birthdays, phone numbers, street names and locations, etc. While we often think of dates and numbers as being less visual than faces or scenery, SJs may use a "photographic" sort of memory to "see" dates, numbers, etc.

With that said, one needn't possess a stellar memory to be an ISJ. Some ISJs sport rather average memories, especially for certain types of information. Some may be better at recalling faces, while others may excel at numeric recall. But considering the amount of time ISJs spend referencing and reflecting on the past, we would certainly expect a strong memory to add greater depth, richness, and quality to their lives.

The Si-Ne Function Pair

Si and Ne always occur together in SJ and NP types, constituting the Si-Ne "function pair." Of course, these functions differ in their respective ordering in the functional stack, with Si being higher and more conscious for SJs and Ne being the more prominent function for NPs.

In combining material conservativism (Si) and mental creativity (Ne), the Si-Ne function pair brings an appetite for resourcefulness and craftiness. Like NPs, when SJs need something, they enjoy using Ne to cleverly fashion it from existing resources (Si) rather than purchasing something new (Se). Regular patrons of thrift shops and craft stores, SJs strive to marry Ne ingenuity with Si minimalism. Their penchant for acting resourcefully helps explain their relative indifference to current fashions. Even fashion-minded ISJs take more of an Ne hodge-podge approach than one of Se trendiness.

The Si-Ne function pair also involves a tension between traditionalism (Si) and unconventionalism (Ne). In SJ types, Si traditionalism typically gains the upper hand, involving careful adherence to existing traditions, worldviews, and methods. They are more concerned with ensuring their beliefs and behaviors align with an existing standard (Si) than with formulating their own unique approach (Ne). Because

Si is less conscious and falls lower in the functional stack for NP types, it is typically less influential. Healthy NPs openly explore a broad array of ideas and lifestyles, both conventional and unconventional. Unlike ISJs, it is not uncommon for NPs to forsake or significantly revise their childhood traditions and worldview.

Lastly, the Ne-Si function pair entails a temporal element, with Si attuning to the past and Ne to future possibilities. While we could certainly argue it less natural and less healthy for ENPs to devote their time and energy to exploring the past, many follow in the footsteps of ISJs and develop strong interests in history. Doing so can feel deeply meaningful to ENPs and ISJs alike, engendering a sense of union between their beliefs (Ne) and past actualities (Si). This seems particularly common among those interested in religion or politics, who seek to root or reinforce their beliefs in the concrete past.

Si vs. Ni

We can also compare and contrast Si with its intuitive cousin, Ni. As we saw in Chapter 6, Si and Ni are both convergent forms of perception. Si takes the entirety of an individual's past and effectively condenses it into a limited set of behavioral preferences. This synoptic past serves as a blueprint for informing present and future behavior.

Ni also functions convergently, synthesizing information to produce insights, impressions, and explanations. While Ni is more concerned with perceiving abstract truths than it is with enacting them, INJs may nonetheless display certain behavioral tendencies that are common to J types. For instance, they generally prefer a certain measure of structure and stability in their lifestyle and living arrangements. Unlike NP types, they aren't open to living like vagabonds, bouncing from one place to the next without any clear plan or purpose.

The most noteworthy Si-Ni difference is that Si fails to apprehend a different reality behind sense data in the way that Ni does. Seeing hidden patterns and discerning causal relationships requires a specific tool (i.e., intuition) that SJs don't enjoy ready access to. This is why ISJs typically rely on traditions and outside authorities (e.g., pundits, clergy, etc.) for insights into hidden N realities. Similarly, INJs may turn to others to compensate for their own shortcomings, such as handling Si details and particulars.

Si & the Brain

According to Dario Nardi's research, ISJs, like INJs, often show strong activation in the visual regions of the brain. From this we might conclude that introverted perception, like extraverted perception, commonly entails a pronounced visual element. Nardi also reports that ISJs display a variety of brain activation patterns, depending on the ISJ's specialty area. In other words, as ISJs develop their own set of habits and interests, their brains respond by structuring themselves accordingly.

In structuring itself around repetition and redundancy, the Si brain is in many respects the opposite of what we see with P types. Because the left side of the brain is commonly associated with stability and redundancy, SJs are often conceived of as more left-brained (although, as we've seen, Si does have certain right-brained features as well). The P brain (not to be confused with "pea brain"), by contrast, reflects a state of openness to new ideas (Ne) or novel stimuli from the environment (Se). Hence, P types are often classified as more right-brained, since the right hemisphere is characteristically more fluid and open.

Chapter 11

EXTRAVERTED SENSING (SE)

Primary roles: To perceive and mediate prompt responses to external details and events; to seek a breadth of novel sensory experiences; to physically interact with the world

Most prominent in: ESTPs & ESFPs; also prominent in ISTPs & ISFPs

Associated with: Sensation-seeking, kinesthetic intelligence, an "eye for detail," attunement to style and appearances, hands-on activities, effortless performance

Famous ESPs: George W. Bush, Lebron James, Beyoncé, Shakira, Donald Trump

Se serves as the dominant function for ESPs and the auxiliary for ISP types. It perceives incoming information by way of the five senses (i.e., sight, smell, taste, sound, and touch).

Since Se is an extraverted function, SPs seek a greater breadth and diversity of sensory experiences than SJ types. They delight in exploring and enjoying the full array of sensory and physical pleasures life has to offer. They relish new tastes, sights, and experiences. Many enjoy cooking and sampling new drinks and cuisines.

SPs are also the most active, "hands-on," and physically engaged of all types. When immersed in a concrete activity, they experience a seamless flow between perception and action, between seeing and doing, between the eyes and the hands. This is why so many SPs enjoy athletics, performance (e.g., singing, dancing, acting, etc.), and a variety of hands-on work.

An Eye for Detail

Like Si, Se is detail-oriented, but in a different sort of way. Si always keeps one eye on the past, comparing present details to pre-existing standards or expectations (e.g., "Is that a new picture on the wall? I don't recall seeing it there before."). Se, by contrast, is less concerned with the way things have or have not changed, and more interested in sensory novelties. It attunes to details it perceives as novel, interesting, or otherwise important. It is constantly scanning the environment for noteworthy sensory novelties, appreciating details that other types tend to gloss over.

As a child, I would occasionally venture on long car rides with my ISTP father. He loved driving because it furnished him ample time for both thinking (Ti) and sightseeing (Se). Over the course of these excursions, he invariably "spotted" things to bring to my attention: a deer prancing through a distant field, a rare or vintage sports car, a circling hawk scoping out its prey. Only rarely did he seem focused on the road ahead, preferring instead to scan the countryside for new and noteworthy sights to behold.

Many SPs also display impressive powers of visual recall. While they may or may not display an innate sense of direction, most are good at recalling landmarks. This is due, at least in part, to their constant attunement to their surroundings. Taking interest in the details of what is happening around them, they are better at recalling contextual details than other types.

Image & Appearance

In attuning to novel sensory details, it is only natural that SPs take note of new styles and fashions. ESPs, in particular, are the most likely of all types to keep pace with current styles. They can't help but take notice of what other people are doing, wearing, driving, etc. They are like mirrors of the material world. Whatever they perceive around them they tend to reflect in their actions, possessions, and lifestyle.

While not all ESTPs dress stylishly, most enjoy sporting new, stylish, or at least well-maintained vehicles. ESFPs are among the most aesthetically-concerned of all types, being highly attentive to their own appearance, as well as that of their surroundings. This, combined with their natural attunement to current styles and fashions, often renders them fashionable and physically attractive. Their homes are typically well-manicured and, budget permitting, embellished with all the latest accoutrements.

In light of the above, ESPs are commonly criticized for being shallow and "superficial." The stone throwers, in this case, are typically introverts (often INs). Despite the fact that all extraverts, not to mention all the extraverted functions, are in a certain sense superficial, Se seems to be one of the easiest and most preferred targets of the introverted critique. More specifically, ESPs are often accused of being too consumed with things like image, status, appearances, and material goods.

The Se-Ni Function Pair

Se and Ni always occur together in SP and NJ types, constituting the Se-Ni function pair. For ESPs, Se is dominant and highly conscious, with Ni being inferior and mostly unconscious. The reverse is true for INJs, for whom Ni is more conscious and Se less conscious.

These inverse functional configurations lead INJs and ESPs to experience the world in dramatically different ways. INJs' typical mode of experiencing the world is impressionistic. They are less inclined to notice or zero-in on concrete details. They are oblivious to details ESPs would readily register. Instead of consciously attending to sensory details, INJs' Se collects them unconsciously and uses them as raw materials for discerning what is happening beneath the surface of things (Ni). So rather than noticing the details of an individual's appearance, for instance, an INJ might be impressed by the degree to which she seems genuine in her presentation.

While Se attends to the appearance of things, Ni is concerned with their deeper qualities and substantiveness. ESPs are constantly acquiring new goods, even if of lower quality, to keep things interesting and trendy. And while INJs are to some extent concerned with appearances (they too have Se), they are more attuned to the quality and craftsmanship of things. They are less concerned about being trendy than ensuring things are substantive, thoughtfully-crafted, and otherwise amenable to their Ni tastes. NFJs, in particular, often exhibit the most refined (or what other types may deem expensive or pretentious) tastes of all types. The popular television comedy, Frasier, is a great example. Much of the show's humor revolves around the sophisticated snobbiness of Frasier (ENFJ) and his brother Niles (INFJ). This includes flaunting linguistic formalisms and a high-brow vocabulary, as well as frequent allusions to fine dining, orchestral music, designer clothing, and the like.

The Ni concern for quality and substance may at times be mistaken for Se image consciousness. For instance, if an INTJ were to purchase an expensive vehicle, such as a Mercedes Benz, some types may view this as an attempt to gain Se style points. But the reasons behind the INTJ's decision may actually have more to do with quality design and engineering (Ni) than with looking trendy or stylish (Se). I have also seen SPs invoke similar Ni justifications in hopes of preempting critiques of their own high-dollar purchases.

Se vs. Ne

Se and Ne share certain similarities. As extraverted perceiving functions, both seek stimulation from, and engagement with, the outside world. Both work broadly rather than narrowly, casting their nets widely so as to maximize their opportunity for diversity and novelty. There is of course a rather important distinction between Se and Ne, namely, the S-N difference. Se deals in the realm of the observable and tangible, while Ne concerns itself with more abstract, ideational matters.

Moreover, Se can be associated, at least to some extent, with conventional lifestyles and appearances, while Ne often ventures off the beaten path. ESPs tend to reflect the material trends around them, mirroring and mimicking whatever is in vogue. While ENPs may be aware of current trends and fashions, they are more apt to put their own unique spin on things. They are more concerned with dressing creatively than with appearing Se trendy. ENPs also show greater openness to unconventional living arrangements, with many being critical of the Se "bourgeois lifestyle."

ENPs are also more flighty, oblivious, and absent-minded than ESPs. Getting lost in their own thoughts and musings, they can appear to have "their head in the clouds." ENPs may also present as teeming with enthusiasm, especially when their Ne is in full throttle. While ESPs are less apt to appear lost in or overly enthusiastic about their thoughts, they often show signs of physical restlessness, such as fidgeting, foot-tapping, looking around, pacing, and so on. This is why both ESPs and ENPs can both be prone to attention-deficit diagnoses. ESPs are more apt to be diagnosed with ADHD (attention-deficit hyperactivity disorder), while ENPs seem disposed to ADD (attention-deficit disorder). In my view, it is not that EPs lack attention per se, but merely require higher levels or certain types of stimulation to fully capture their attention.

Se vs. Si

Se and Si are similar in their concern for details and concrete matters. While Se attends to environmental details, Si is concerned with recalling or reconciling past details with those of the present. Se gathers concrete information broadly, seeking diversity and novelty. Si perceives more narrowly, drawing on past experiences, especially those which have become routinized or otherwise deeply engrained.

The sensing functions can also be associated with lifestyle preferences—food, housing, material goods, spending habits, and so on. As we've seen, types using Si (NPs and SJs) tend to be more conservative in their approach to material goods. They pride themselves in creatively recycling and reusing material resources whenever possible.

Types using Se (SPs and NJs) are more liberal in their expenditures. Remember, Se is concerned with securing a breadth of sensory experiences. And one surefire way of doing so is purchasing material goods or novel experiences (e.g., vacations, dining out, etc.).

Se types are also more concerned with physical appearances, which often translates into time spent improving or stylizing their own appearance or possessions. Female SPs and NJs, for instance, seem more inclined to spend time applying make-up than SJ or NP females. Geographically speaking, Los Angeles and Beverly Hills are apt examples of the Se-Ni lifestyle, while northwestern cities such as San Francisco, Portland, and Seattle are characteristically Ne-Si.

With that said, Se-Si differences may be less overt in ESJs and ISPs, since their dominant E-I attitude may serve to moderate their Si or Se auxiliary. Conditioning and circumstances can also have a moderating effect. I have known, for instance, ISPs who by many standards would qualify as "savers," as well as ESJs who would qualify as "spenders." With that said, if we zoom out and look at the general patterns, Si-Se differences still hold in ESJs and ISPs, even if less consistent or obvious than what we see in ESPs and ISJs.

Se & the Brain

According to Dario Nardi, SPs exhibit what he calls a "tennis-hop" brain pattern. In using the term "tennis-hop," he is referencing a common practice among tennis players, involving a side-to-side hopping motion as they await a serve or returned ball from their opponent. Nardi suggests that SPs' brain activity assumes this sort of pattern as they await new stimuli from the environment. The tennis-hop pattern is asymmetrical and oscillating, which Nardi believes primes them for quick sensorimotor responses. He reports that all personality types display this pattern during certain activities, such as while playing video games requiring quick hand-eye responses.

You may recall that the "Christmas tree" pattern, characteristic of the Ne brain, was also asymmetrical. The asymmetric activity displayed in both Se and Ne brain states seems consistent with the random, impulsive, and unpredictable ways of P types. It seems that Mother Nature has wired P types (especially EPs) to await or seek new ideas, experiences, or possibilities to which they can readily respond and adapt.

Chapter 12

INTRODUCTED THINKING (TI)

Primary role: To examine practical or conceptual issues using deep, implicit, and nuanced logic; to develop and refine subjective methods, strategies, or concepts

Most prominent in: INTPs & ISTPs. Also prominent in ENTPs & ESTPs

Associated with: Deep skepticism, tacit logic, self-regulation and self-optimization, personal independence and autonomy

Famous ITPs: Einstein, Bill Gates, Henri Bergson, Robert Pirsig, Robert Nozick, Ken Wilber, Lance Armstrong

ITPs use Ti as their dominant function, while ETPs use it as their auxiliary. Ti applies deep logic and nuanced reasoning to understand practical or conceptual issues. Unlike the more standardized and systematic ways of Te, Ti has more of an intuitive, right-brained flavor. While it can certainly be applied to more formal or structured problems, such as mathematical proofs or philosophical syllogisms, it is more of a free-wheeling sort of logic that is typically applied informally.

According to Dario Nardi, one of the roles of Ti is integrating visual and kinesthetic data. More specifically, Nardi associates it with "object identification and motor skills, such as aim…it helps us determine where we end and the rest of the world begins." Along similar lines, Lenore Thomson, in her book, *Personality Type*, suggests that Ti predominates in activities like aligning and hammering a nail. In determining where and how hard to strike the nail, Ti uses a technique commonly known as "eyeballing." It informally assesses the situation (e.g., the size of the hammer, length of the nail, thickness of the board) and proceeds to make judgments and adjustments for each successive strike of the nail. Through this sort of informal reasoning, TPs develop their own unique methods and techniques, many of which may significantly differ from those of other TPs. This is why Ti methods are often described as "subjective." Unlike Te methods, they are not standardized or collectively determined.

Subjective Methods & Strategies

TPs enjoy developing and refining their own methods and techniques. Such techniques may be characteristically N (e.g., writing, philosophizing) or S (e.g., athletic skills, mechanical / technical skills, etc.) in nature. Unlike ISJs, ITPs despise working in a cookie-cutter, step-by-step fashion. Eschewing instruction manuals and "how-to" guides whenever possible, they prefer to use their own methods and powers of reasoning to figure things out.

A great example of Ti working in tandem with both S and N can be found in Robert Pirsig's classic philosophical novel, *Zen and the Art of Motorcycle Maintenance*. Written from the first-person perspective, the ITP narrator recounts his thoughts and experiences over the course of a cross-country motorcycle trip, a trip whose express purpose involved achieving philosophical and existential clarity. One of the beautiful things about the book is Pirsig's ability to interweave S and N elements. As intimated by the book's title, his experiences with motorcycle repair (S) illustrate and inform his philosophical insights (N). While Pirsig's musings are certainly interesting from a philosophical perspective, they also constitute a lucid and accessible first-hand look at Ti in action. Pirsig's thought processes, as well as his descriptions of how to properly maintain a motorcycle, wonderfully portray the subjective methods of Ti, not to mention its philosophical propensities. Interestingly, Pirsig's philosophy and his method of motorcycle maintenance dovetail in a concept he calls "quality." He suggests the notion of quality cannot be fully captured in words, which is unsurprising in light of what we know about Ti's status as a more tacit form of reasoning.

In addition to formulating its own subjective methods, Ti also develops and refines its own strategies. It is constantly making calculations based on numerous variables (again, typically informally) in order to maximize efficiency and achieve its objectives. For example, an ITP concerned with maximizing fuel economy might use Ti to calibrate his speed and minimize brake usage while driving (i.e., "hypermiling"). Or, he may consider clever ways of consolidating trips or tasks to maximize efficiency. Such strategies are rarely explicated in a way that a business plan might be. Explicit and carefully delineated strategies are more consistent with Te methodology. Ti strategies are more impromptu and makeshift, allowing for fluid calibration to the situation at hand. A Ti hunter, for instance, might constantly adjust his strategy in response to ever changing circumstances. The same could be said for Ti athletes over the course of an athletic contest.

Deep Skepticism & Reductive Thinking

ITPs are constantly examining their own thoughts to scrutinize their logic and better understand their origins. They consider it unacceptable to construct a theory on a dubious conceptual platform. Their insistence on developing a pure and logical foundation makes them less confident than J types about what can be considered "fact" or "knowledge." Indeed, many TPs, especially NTPs, are unsure we can know much of anything with full confidence. Many of the ancient "sophists" may well have been NTPs, not to mention a hefty chunk of contemporary "postmodernists." Robert Pirsig, who we discussed above, found much to like in the ancient sophists.

Ti can readily identify inconsistencies or logical shortcomings in nearly any line of reasoning. TPs find it easier to identify inconsistencies or logical shortcomings—to assert what *isn't true*— than to confidently assert *what is*. Due to Ti's acute sensitivity to logical inconsistencies, TPs can be quick (sometimes too quick) to dismiss entire theories, throwing out the proverbial baby with the bathwater. J types, by contrast, seem less deterred by ostensible inconsistencies, perhaps figuring they will eventually be explained or reconciled.

When it comes to building a system of knowledge, Ti's first priority is to identify and clarify the lowest common denominator. It works to strip away all "non-essentials." It then proceeds to represent and describe what is essential by way of concepts. NTPs, in particular, derive great joy from playing with concepts. They love developing, refining, and scrutinizing them. They may even utilize charts and diagrams in hopes of maximizing the coherency, consistency, and structure of their concepts and frameworks. Their thirst for foundational knowledge in the form of concepts contributes to their penchant for philosophy and philosophizing.

Although NJs and NFPs also feel at home with concepts, they are typically not as enamored with them as NTPs seem to be. NTJs, for instance, seem concerned with describing and understanding *systems* than with exploring and refining the concepts themselves. For INTJs, concepts are important insofar as they contribute to a better understanding of the system. For NTPs, however, the concepts themselves are celebrated as forums for employing Ti logic and exploring Ne associations. The personality preferences and functions described in this book are examples of the sorts of concepts NTPs enjoy wrestling with.

Control, Freedom, & Autonomy

Because Ti is an introverted judging function, ITPs can in many respects be considered "inner control freaks." Even if seeing themselves as outwardly adaptable or easygoing, their need to be in control of themselves is most apparent when others try to instruct, manage, or in any way coerce them. When ITPs sense that others are trying to control them, they instinctively resist or retract. There may be nothing they despise more than being controlled from without.

In light of their thirst for self-control, ITPs are highly concerned with maximizing their freedom and autonomy; they are the most fiercely independent of all types. They want to do things their own way and in their own time. They resist, even if only inwardly, any actual or perceived threat to their autonomy. For similar reasons, they may gravitate toward anarchist or libertarian political philosophies.

These same dynamics animate ITPs' religious preferences. Namely, their first inclination is to shuck all authority. For INTPs in particular, this often makes theism an unacceptable option, which is why many INTPs consider themselves atheists or agnostics. It's not that they forsake theism without some objective reasons for doing so, but Ti, especially when combined with Ne, predisposes ITPs to explore and embrace anti-theistic arguments. INTPs can be so hell-bent on being free and independent that they don't want to be accountable to anyone or anything, including a god or deity.

Nor are TPs (especially INTPs) particularly willing to cede their independence in the workplace. Capitulating to standardized policies, procedures, and protocols (i.e., Te rules) is anathema to them; standardization runs against their grain. TPs thrive on having the freedom to develop and employ their own approach. All of this makes them reluctant to function as employees and curious about entrepreneurship. Many ITPs decide they would rather pave their own path and risk financial instability than die a slow death among organizational rules and bureaucracy.

When TPs do find themselves part of a system, many can't help but push the envelope to see how much freedom they can carve out for themselves, calculating ways of abnegating or circumventing as many Te responsibilities as possible (this, again, is most pronounced in INTPs). They do this because they are naturally repelled by external systems of control (Te), which feel too far removed from the more instinctive ways of Ti. Just as Fe norms can feel dehumanizing from the perspective of Fi individualism, excessive Te rules can be seen as dehumanizing ITPs by stripping them of their freedom to use their dominant function.

TPs' thirst for autonomy also carries huge implications for their relationships. This is especially true for ITPs, who struggle to reconcile their Ti's push for complete independence with their inferior Fe's need for social affiliation and affirmation. Whether they are willing to admit it or not, ITPs have a "need to be needed." Deep down, most are terrified of being alone, feeling that their sense of purpose and motivation will evaporate without someone else in their lives. With that said, there are times when ITPs feel so self-sufficient and independent that they convince themselves they don't need other people. But after droughts of human interaction, they invariably start to feel something missing from their lives. This prompts them to reinitiate contact with others, at least until they feel compelled to assert their independence again.

Their penchant for independence also influences ITPs' approach to others' ideas. Namely, they have great difficulty accepting much of anything as true unless it resonates with their own logic or is confirmed in their own experience. They seem to lack faith in anyone's logic but their own. While open to hearing and entertaining others' perspectives, when it comes to making decisions about what is or isn't true, Ti is the ultimate arbiter. With that said, ITPs may be more open to accepting outside opinions regarding certain F matters (e.g., what constitutes good art, music, style, etc.), which fall outside the purview of Ti logic.

Ti & the Brain

According to Dario Nardi's research, TPs exhibit strong use of four brain regions responsible for complex logical reasoning. While other types may show activation in one or two of these regions, TPs commonly display concurrent activation in two to four of them. Nardi suggests this allows TPs to effectively:

- Linearly derive solutions (left side of brain)
- Holistically work with concepts (right side)
- Integrate visual-kinesthetic data (left side)
- Weigh pros and cons of competing factors or options (right side)

Nardi's findings also confirm ITPs' reputed propensity for detachment. Namely, he found that ITPs are adept at drowning out background noise in order to enhance concentration and objectivity. They can focus and "get in the zone" even in noisy or otherwise distracting environments. This ability to "tune out the world" allows them to better focus on their thoughts and projects.

Not only can Ti shut down external noise, but also internal emotional noise. Little is more distracting or unsettling to TPs than experiencing negative emotions. When negative emotions are running high, TPs lose their usual sense of self-control. This often leads them to experiment with cognitive, behavioral, and philosophical techniques to preempt or mitigate negative emotions.

To learn more about Ti, be sure to explore my books, *The INTP* and *The INTP Quest*.

Chapter 13

EXTRAVERTED THINKING (TE)

Primary roles: To succinctly express logic-based judgments; to understand or render systems and operations more rational, efficient, and effective

Most prominent in: ENTJs & ESTJs; also prominent in INTJs & ISTJs

Associated with: Explicit logic, precise and pointed expressions, bureaucracy and "red tape," quantitative methods ("Show me the numbers!")

Famous ETJs: Henry Ford, Bill O'Reily

ETJ types use Extraverted Thinking (Te) as their dominant function, while ITJs employ it as their auxiliary. As an extraverted function, Te is readily identifiable in the presentation and expressions of TJ types. It is characteristically impersonal, focused more on things and systems than people or feelings. TJs readily express their rational judgments; they literally think (i.e., make logical judgments, conclusions, and decisions) aloud. Their direct, "to the point" style is sometimes perceived by others as harsh, blunt, or tactless. Physicians with poor bedside manner, such as Dr. House of the acclaimed television show *House*, are notorious for their Te brusqueness.

TJs strive to make the external world and its operations more rational. Toward this end, they often end up managing businesses or organizations. ENTJs, in particular, are highly represented among CEOs, with ESTJs and ISTJs gobbling up the middle-level management positions. While INTJs may also float to the top of organizations, as Ni dominants, they typically prefer the role of senior advisor to that of manager or decision-maker.

TJs may also be drawn to various teaching and training roles. I have personally encountered numerous ISTJ elementary school teachers, and research has shown INTJs to be quite common among college professors. Generally speaking, TJs enjoy work that allows them to order, organize, and manage information or operations.

In my experience, TJ males are often more extreme in their Te presentation (i.e., more characteristically "left-brained") than TJ females. This relates to what we saw in Chapter 5, namely, that males generally enjoy less balance and communication between brain hemispheres. Hence, some of the material presented in this chapter, designed to paint a distinct portrait of Te, may fail to fully resonate with some TJ females.

Defining & Measuring

Te approaches and structures things in explicitly rational ways. It may do so for the sake of understanding (e.g., science), utility (e.g., technology), or maintaining external order (e.g., instating laws and rules). Unlike Ti, whose logic holistically consults both sides of the brain, Te hails squarely from the left hemisphere. The "left brain" is characteristically logical, analytical, systematic, and explicit in its workings. It takes the perceived world, carves it up into small pieces, then proceeds to name and analyze each piece on its own terms.

TJs (especially NTJs) view the world as comprised of myriad systems, each of which can be analyzed and explicated in terms of rational hierarchies. The better each system is understood and rationally delineated, the more amenable it becomes to prediction, control, and manipulation. Since modern science is founded on these Te ideals, it is readily embraced and defended by TJ types.

Never vague or ambiguous, Te employs precise definitions, policies, plans, and procedures. It carefully spells out how to get from here to there, using as many maps, labels, and directions as necessary. From the ETJ perspective, nothing can be optimized unless we work to objectively understand it and control it with standard operating procedures. Such standards should always be clearly explicated to minimize ambiguity and the potential for interpretative error.

Quantification is another hallmark feature of the Te approach. This may involve employing any number of objective measurements, benchmarks, statistics, and the like. The increasingly popular notion of "evidenced-based practice" is a good example, which in most cases is synonymous with quantitative research. For TJs, more than other types, the "numbers don't lie." They believe that formal quantitative research should serve as the bedrock of human knowledge and decision-making.

As an example of the Te proclivity for formal testing, my INTJ friend is always prodding me to implement "split testing" on various pages of my blog. Essentially, a split test is like a miniature science experiment. It involves setting up two nearly identical pages with only minor differences (e.g., a different color or layout). Half of the blog visitors are then directed to one page, while the other half is served the alternate page. Statistics are then used to determine which variation performs better.

The Te-Fi Function Pair

Te and Fi always occur together in TJs and FPs, constituting the Te-Fi function pair. For TJs, Te is the more conscious and Fi the less conscious function, while the reverse is true for FP types. Although Te and Fi are in some respects functional opposites, they are also complementary.

Fi, as we will see in the next chapter, evaluates and refines personal tastes, feelings, and values. It champions individuality, emphasizing and defending the unique qualities of the individual. It shows particular concern for life's "underdogs"—children, animals, the elderly, the underserved, and so on.

Because of the highly rational presentation of Te and the introverted nature of Fi, it can be easy to assume that TJs are devoid of emotion. But their outward presentation belies the fact that TJs can experience deep feelings and develop strong attachments via their Fi. Like IFPs, some TJs are sensitive to instances of injustice, inequity, and victimization. Both TJs and FPs are inclined to turn to legislation (Te) for redressing perceived injustices or victimization (Fi). We see this all the time, for instance, when Fi tragedies (e.g., school shootings, child abductions) prompt the passing of new laws or the formation of new organizations (Te) intended to prevent future recurrences.

From this we learn of the typological connection between deep personal feelings (Fi) and collective rules and policies (Te). The notion of a "fair and just" system or workplace aptly illustrates this Fi-Te connection. Science fiction is another good example, exploring the effects of technology (Te) on individual experiences and values (Fi). This, by the way, is why science fiction junkies are often TJ or FP types.

Te vs. Ti

Compared to Te, Ti is a more implicit and subjective form of logic. Rather than looking outward and referencing objective standards, it reasons and operates according to its own inner criteria. It also spends ample time questioning underlying premises and assumptions, desperately seeking, but struggling to find, firm epistemological footing. It therefore tends to be more critical and reductive in its workings.

Te, by contrast, is more positivistic and forward-moving (especially in ETJs), constantly proposing new facts, definitions, policies, procedures, and so on. Indeed, we see this sort of expansiveness with all the extraverted functions. The extraverted functions are constantly adding and broadening, while the introverted functions tend to reduce and deepen. So while Te goes about expanding the number of T assertions in the world, Ti earns its keep by scrutinizing, undercutting, or circumventing them.

One can find this Te-Ti tension in nearly any organization. Those on the Te side are always looking for ways to improve operations, which often involves developing and implementing new policies and procedures. Meanwhile, those in the Ti corner are pushing to keep things open-ended in the name of individual autonomy. We see similar tensions in political discourse, such as debates over limited government (Ti) versus government expansion (Te).

Te, as we've seen, also aligns itself with "the scientific method," or, more broadly, with objective methods. Some TJs (as well as FPs), put science on a pedestal, seeing it as humanity's primary hope for ultimate knowledge or salvation. While obtaining knowledge and solving the problems of humanity are also of interest to TPs, they prefer to approach these matters less formally on the individual level. They feel that individuals can discover truth and wisdom through their own minds, methods, and experiences. This of course exemplifies the age-old distinction between the scientist (Te) and the philosopher (Ti or Ni).

Te & the Brain

We've already discussed how Te primarily draws on the left side of the brain, which is predominantly analytical and impersonal in its workings. More specifically, Dario Nardi's research suggests that Te can be associated with the following characteristics:

- Use of "evidence-based" reasoning and practices

- Reliance on measurable sensory information

- Oriented toward goals and task completion

- Propensity for quick, efficient action (sometimes to the detriment of accuracy)

Nardi also associates Te with efficient utilization of brain resources. Namely, when TJs are making decisions or working toward an objective, only the bare minimum number of brain regions tends to show activity; everything else is shut down. This includes quieting emotional activity that could feasibly slow or otherwise complicate the ETJ's work. Nardi suggests this neurological efficiency allows ETJs (and perhaps other types using Te) to quickly and effortlessly make judgments and decisions, without much in the way of mental fatigue. This helps explain their propensity and ability to function effectively as managers and executives.

When vacationing from their typical Te mode of operation, Nardi suggests that TJs can show high activity in a brain region responsible for handling personal values. This region, located on the right side of the brain, is characteristically negative in its affective evaluations (e.g., "That's stupid!" or "That's morally reprehensible!"). This, of course, points to TJs' use of Fi, providing empirical confirmation that Te and Fi occur together as a function pair.

Chapter 14

INTRODUCED FEELING (FI)

Primary roles: To explore and refine personal tastes, feelings, and values, contributing to a strong sense of personal uniqueness; to maintain inner emotional and moral order; to emotionally invest in a limited number of persons, animals, or interests

Most prominent in: INFPs & ISFPs; also prominent in ENFPs & ESFPs

Associated with: Fighting for "underdogs," emotional restraint, nuanced morals and values, nurture and caregiving, sensitivity to perceived inequities and injustice

Famous IFPs: Henry David Thoreau, Jean-Jacque Rousseau, Kierkegaard, Camus, Virginia Wolfe, Van Gogh, Luke Skywalker, J.D. Salinger, Jane Austen, Bob Dylan

IFPs use Fi as their dominant function, while EFPs wield it as their auxiliary. Fi is an introverted judging function. Like the other introverted functions, it is characteristically intensive rather than extensive. Rather than surveying and distributing feelings across a breadth of individuals (as Fe does), Fi focuses largely on one's own feelings and sentiments. While FJs routinely turn to others for emotional support, FPs explore and manage their emotions on a largely independent basis.

Fi is also less concerned with cultivating group morale or consensus of feeling than Fe is. While FPs may invest in the well-being of select individuals (e.g., their children), Fi is not authentically concerned with, nor does it feel responsible for, the overall feeling tenor of groups.

FPs empathize with, and form attachments to, things that move or personally affect them—their pets, their children, the needy, etc. The scope of Fi attachments is typically narrower than that of Fe, limited to a select number of individuals, interests, or causes. FPs may invest a great deal of time and emotional energy in a single individual, contributing to their value as parents, caregivers, therapists, tutors, etc.

FPs can often be found helping those deemed unable to help themselves—children, animals, the sick, the needy, the elderly, and so on. They love to rescue those in need, such as feeding stray animals or adopting pets from animal shelters. They also take up niche causes that have personally impacted them, such as raising awareness about a rare disease affecting a loved one.

Being outwardly receptive and non-judgmental, IFPs can serve as veritable dumping grounds for others' emotional baggage. For some IFPs, this engenders a deep sense of emotional burden, as well as a melancholic attitude toward life.

Constrained Feeling

Since Fi is introverted in direction, IFPs, in particular, may not even look like feelers when viewed from without. Outside of wielding their more playful Se or Ne auxiliary, IFPs can seem cool, indifferent, aloof, and uninviting. Giving little evidence of feeling in their intonations or facial expressions, some may even be accused of "lacking personality."

While all introverts may at times seem aloof or detached, those without Fe (e.g., IFPs and ITJs) are more apt to be charged with lacking personality. Of course, such critiques are typically unwarranted, since we know that the inner world of IFPs is rich, complex, and animated with feeling. It may require certain circumstances, such as engaging with pets, children, etc., for IFPs' emotions to overflow into outward expression. Even then, they still appear more constrained than what we see in FJ types.

While the constraining influence of Fi may contribute to perceptions of IFPs being aloof or indifferent, it may also be viewed, at least by some, as a more "mature" way of handling emotions. Its extraverted alternative, Fe, expresses emotions more readily, laying everything out on the emotional table. Compared to Fi, Fe may seem needy, melodramatic, or attention-seeking. And since FJs lean more on others for emotional support, some may see them, rightly or wrongly, as less mature in handling their emotions.

Refining Tastes & Values

Fi also works to shape its own worldview, one that can serve as a platform for self-understanding, self-direction, and independent decision-making. In this sense, it resembles Ti, which involves a similar process of developing and refining an inner map. This structuring process (i.e., inner judging), contributing to a sense of inner order and personal identity, was nicely illustrated by one of my INFP blog contributors:

> *"My inner values and feelings (Fi) are like a building, a structure of affections that inform my worldview. This involves an inner love for certain things, and an inner repulsion for other things. My values and feelings form "blocks" of varying hardness, depending on how strongly I feel about them; the stronger ones are more resilient...I constantly discover more about the structure as I go, and what I should change to make it better. For*

example, I didn't have to factually discern a respect for human
dignity; I simply found myself in situations where people did not
respect human dignity, and it made me angry — I found out
that I hated bullying."

IFPs explore and refine this inner structure of tastes and values through art, reading, music, films, caregiving, journaling, creative writing, and so on. As they refine and develop their tastes, values, and beliefs, they grow in their self-understanding and clarify what really matters to them.

Inner Control

Like ITPs, IFPs feel they have little control over other people or the outside world. They are inclined to feel, with Aldous Huxley, that "there is only one corner of the universe you can be certain of improving, and that's your own self." It is therefore important that IFPs feel in control of themselves and their lives. Indeed, this is partly why they invest so much time and effort into exploring their feelings and clarifying their identity. They want to figure out who they are so they can effectively be themselves.

While IFPs may see themselves as outwardly adaptable or easygoing, they may be somewhat blind to the degree to which they need or seek control. This is most clearly evidenced when they perceive others as trying to control or emotionally manipulate them, to which they instinctively resist or retract. This helps explain IFPs' reputation for not answering their phones and their strong preference for texting. Texting affords them time to formulate an authentic response without concern for being "put on the spot" or emotionally manipulated into doing something they don't want to do.

Since IFPs feel most in control when alone, periods of solitude are of great importance to them. Being alone allows them to let down their guard and catch their breath. It gives them the space they need to freely explore their feelings and interests.

Marginalized & Misunderstood

IFPs can feel overrun by the fast-paced, cut-throat ways of modern society. Their propensity for feeling personally victimized may contribute to their sense of empathy for society's victims and underlings. INFPs, in particular, may struggle with the world's ostensible indifference to the "impractical" NF gifts they have to offer; the notion of the "starving artist" may seem like a real possibility for many INFP creatives. Like INFJs, they may see themselves as chronically misunderstood, leading to "misfit" or "outsider" self-conceptions. Many INFPs turn to music, writing, or art as ways of exploring and expressing their feelings of being marginalized or misunderstood.

Of course, not all IFPs feel like outcasts. INFPs who spend much of their time engrossed in Fi and Te, showing minimal use or development of their auxiliary Ne, tend to look and feel more "normal" than the more artsy or subversive INFPs. Of all the FP types, ESFPs are typically the most conventional and least ideationally "deviant," not to mention the most at home in the world. As sensors, ISFPs are also less otherworldly and therefore less apt to feel marginalized.

Combatting Injustice & Defending Individuality

FPs often see outer circumstances (Te) as playing a prominent role in individual suffering (Fi). FPs are more sensitive to instances of perceived inequity, injustice, or victimization than other types. Not only are they sensitive to the role of unfortunate circumstances in others' suffering, but also their own. Many recount an instance or period of abuse or injustice that they see as having left an indelible imprint on their lives. IFPs seem slower to let go of these things than other types, often using them as emotional fuel for their life's purpose. An IFP victim of rape or molestation, for instance, may funnel her hurt and anger toward reducing the incidence of rape and related sex offenses. Because of IFPs' tendency to remember or hold onto past emotional pain, they can have a tragic or melancholic air about them (this seems much rarer among EFPs).

FPs can also be quite sensitive to instances of perceived discrimination or stereotyping. Even personality typing can be viewed as threatening by certain FP individuals wary of being stripped of their personal uniqueness (e.g., "Don't try to put me in a box or pigeonhole me!"). In other words, because Fi celebrates and defends the tastes, feelings, and values that make each person special, any attempt at reducing them to a common denominator can feel offensive and dehumanizing. We see the same line of reasoning among Fi anthropologists concerned with preserving the unique attributes of various tribes and cultures, poised to defend them against the homogenizing forces of globalization.

Fi vs. Ti

As introverted judging functions, Fi and Ti share much in common. Both confer a sense of inner order and structure, both are intensive and intentional, and both involve a more subjective or individualized form of judging.

Generally speaking, Fi and Ti work to prevent individual preferences and methods from being swallowed up by collective systems and approaches. They thus serve as important and necessary counterbalances to Fe and Te power structures. Ti counters the bureaucracies and standardized methods of Te, while Fi rallies against the homogenizing social and moral forces of Fe. Since IFPs use Te in addition to Fi, they are typically more tolerant of standardized methods and institutions than ITPs tends to be. Like TJ types, FPs can appreciate (or at least tolerate) external systems that feel orderly and rational. This helps explain why FPs far outnumber TPs among office and administrative staff. Rather than revolting against Te systems, IFPs are more inclined to resist Fe conventions and social niceties, especially those conflicting with their sense of personal authenticity. They may, for instance, refuse to put on a "happy face" when they're not feeling happy, or to feign warmth or friendliness toward individuals they don't really know or respect. Schmoozing or socializing for its own sake is typically frowned upon by IFPs.

ITPs and IFPs are also alike in their tendency to see their own preferences as worthy of wide-scale adoption. They may believe that if others would only follow their example that the world could be greatly improved. ITPs may dream of universalizing their Ti methods and strategies, while IFPs may conjure utopian visions exemplifying their Fi values. These sorts of collective aspirations are ironic in light of IPs' own resistance to externally-imposed methods or directives.

Ti and Fi also differ in some important ways. While IFPs are moved to help the sick, needy, or disenfranchised, TPs shy away from routine helping or caretaking. IFPs also take interest in art, poetry, fiction, music, and the like, while ITPs gravitate toward strategic, conceptual, scientific, or technical pursuits. Of course, these lines can at times be blurred by the inferior function, which, for better or worse, may prompt IFPs to pursue T interests and ITPs to pursue F ones.

Fi & the Brain

According to Dario Nardi, IFPs (especially INFPs) are among the most empathetic listeners. More specifically, he associates Fi with:

- Holistic listening
- Attending to withheld information, i.e., being curious about what others are really thinking or feeling
- Ranking or prioritizing things according to their perceived value
- Diminished activity in brain regions associated with logic

Despite their heavy reliance on Fi judgments, Nardi reports that IFPs can also invoke left-brained logic in their decision-making (Te). So if they find themselves in a pinch, when decisions needs to be made, IFPs may turn to Te, which, as we've seen, is capable of making decisions with remarkable speed, firmness, and efficiency.

Chapter 15

EXTRAVERTED FEELING (FE)

Primary roles: To survey a breadth of human emotions, values, and morals, striving toward interpersonal or group consensus; to directly express feelings and judgments; to instruct or motivate others toward growth and excellence

Most prominent in: ENFJs & ESFJs; also prominent in INFJs & ISFJs

Associated with: An interpersonal focus, emotional expressiveness, communication skills, talkativeness, attunement to social norms, advice-giving

Famous EFJs: Dr. Martin Luther King, Dr. Phil McGraw, Frasier Crane (television)

Fe serves as the dominant function for EFJs and the auxiliary for IFJs. Numerically second to only NPs and NJs, FJs are among the rarer personality types. They do appear more common, however, among African-American females.

EFJs are animated, talkative, assertive, and persuasive. They are the kings and queens of social affairs, capable of quickly reading and establishing rapport with others. Because of their social intelligence and love for people, EFJs develop networks of friends, acquaintances, and social connections.

The Interpersonal Nature of Fe

Fe plays a prominent role in attuning to and empathizing with others' emotions. It reads and recreates others' emotional states, allowing FJs to feel what others are feeling. Knowing what others are feeling is of great importance to FJs, who place high value on establishing emotional rapport and mutual understanding. In short, they want everyone to be on the same emotional page.

The pleasure derived from cultivating rapport contributes to FJs' propensity for supporting and counseling others. NFJs, in particular, see it as their job to help others live more ethically, healthily, and authentically. Utilizing their insight into people, they identify problems and formulate solutions that promote growth and healing. And because NFJs are verbally persuasive, others often respond well to their counsel. This is especially true of those actually seeking their assistance, since FJs can be inclined to dole out unsolicited advice.

Meeting others' needs and maintaining interpersonal harmony are also important to FJs. Feeling responsible for the well-being of others, they work hard to ensure that people are getting along and that their needs are met. Toward this end, they can be self-sacrificing, deferring their own needs for the sake of others. From this we learn that, more than any other function, Fe is *interpersonal* in nature. In many respects, FJs are unable to think only of themselves. At least in theory, they are the least self-focused of all the types (especially EFJs).

Despite their interest in orchestrating social harmony, FJs also feel it important to directly express their own feelings and opinions. After all, Fe is an extraverted judging function. Unlike FPs, who tend to bottle-up and handle their emotions on an independent basis, FJs' natural style is to deal with their emotions out in the open. And because their words are often bathed in emotion, FJs can seem intense and dramatic in their expressions. While other types may view them as somewhat irrational or melodramatic, Fe expressions are rational in the sense of conveying the nature and strength of the experienced emotion. Moreover, because Fe is fairly rare, people often wrongly assume FJs to be more upset than they really are. In many cultures, people are simply not accustomed to encountering strong, feeling-laden expressions.

Fe can present differently among strangers than it does with intimates. At least in many American social settings, FJs feel compelled to be "positive" in their demeanor and expressions, to put on a "happy face." In the company of close confidants, however, FJs feel they can drop the social façade and express their complaints and grievances. Indeed, expressing their feelings via Fe is critical to FJs' psychological (and physical) health. Even if doing so fails to furnish an immediate solution to the problem at hand, they tend to feel better once they have aired their feelings, be it through words or tears. Therefore, healthy FJs invariably have at least one reliable friend or confidant with whom they can openly and candidly express their concerns, opinions, and grievances.

Fe & Social Norms

As is true of Te, there is a certain formalness to Fe. Namely, Fe is highly attuned to social norms and conventions, using these as benchmarks for appropriate social behavior. This may include considering what is appropriate to bring, wear, or say under a given set of social conditions. Notions such as tact, manners, and social grace are examples of Fe norms.

With that said, it is also important to recognize that Fe norms and customs will vary by culture. Hence, there is a universal as well as a culturally-specific aspect to Fe. The universal aspect involves a concern for others and for establishing feeling consensus in the social and moral spheres. Religious proselytizing is one such example, which involves the promotion of what are viewed as universal, God-ordained moral laws.

The Fe-Ti Function Pair

Fe and Ti comprise a single function pair, employed by FJ as well as TP types. The Fe-Ti function pair fosters a tension between self (Ti) and others (Fe), as well as inner control (Ti) and outer control (Fe).

For TPs, Ti is the more conscious member of the function pair. Because of its predominance, TPs see themselves as independent agents with a strong sense of inner control. At the same time, they tend to wither without some degree of social contact (Fe), an experience which prompts their participation in relationships, team sports, fraternities, country clubs, etc. In each of these arenas, we see droves of TPs (typically males) who, while relishing their Ti work, also enjoy rubbing elbows with their comrades in a brotherly sort of way. Hence, there is a certain superficiality to TPs' use of Fe.

Fe is far more developed and nuanced in FJs than it is in TPs. Due to its higher position in the functional stack, FJs show strong differentiation of their Fe. Their capacity to experience and distinguish a wide variety of feeling tones is vast. While TPs may aspire to refine their Fe, they are more amateurish in their Fe capacities, devoid of the natural skill and grace displayed by FJs. In a similar fashion, FJs may work to develop their capacity for Ti logic, but may never approach the level of mastery naturally available to TP types.

Fe and Ti also contribute to control issues. While ITPs typically feel they have little control over the outside world, the inner order granted by their Ti confers a strong sense of self-control. EFJs, by contrast, don't enjoy the luxury of inner control, relying instead on their Fe to procure a sense of outer control. With that said, there are times when these types are tempted to extend their reach of control. ITPs may be tempted to assume leadership positions, while EFJs may take measures to feel more in control of themselves. If and when such attempts fall flat, these types revert back to their natural modes of operating.

Fe vs. Te

As we've seen, Te involves the use of standardized, collective methods (e.g., the scientific method, "evidenced-based" thinking, etc.) in hopes of making the world and its operations more rational. Fe resembles Te in its concern for collective standards. But rather than concerning itself with T matters, it focuses on F standards, such as shared values, morals, and social practices. While Fe standards may differ by culture, as well as by group size (e.g., family, community, nation, etc.), they all privilege the needs of the collective over those of the individual.

In addition to the different aims of their standardizing efforts, Fe and Te also differ in the tone and manner of their expressions. While the content of Fe expressions need not be emotional, there is a discernible difference in their packaging compared to those of Te. Namely, Te can present as rather dry, lifeless, and monotonal. Its purpose is to relay information in an explicit and literal fashion. Fe expressions, by contrast, are often infused with feeling and inflection. Their tone is rich, full, and colorful. The most persuasive of all types, FJs have the power to move and motivate us. Even if the content of their message is not profound or earth-shattering, its emotional packaging can render it powerful and convincing. While Te expressions may be more precise and exacting (e.g., a scientific lecture), those of Fe are more stirring and inspiring (e.g., a moving speech).

Fe vs. Fi

Fe works broadly and extensively, while Fi penetrates more deeply and intensively. Fe is more concerned with collective morale, while Fi focuses more on the feelings of the self or a select few individuals. Like FJs, FPs tend to prefer external harmony, but this is more reflective of their personal discomfort with conflict (i.e., their own disquieting feelings) than of a genuine concern for interpersonal harmony.

The following scenario is sometimes useful for differentiating Fi and Fe. Imagine you are involved in a social gathering, hosted by someone else, involving six couples, three of which are new to the group. Now ask yourself the following questions:

- Would I feel responsible for ensuring that the newer couples feel comfortable and at ease?

- Would I go out of my way to reach out to them and help them assimilate to the group?

- Is helping newcomers feel welcome and comfortable in social settings one of my natural skills?

Generally speaking, FJs answer "yes" to each of the above questions, whereas FPs (especially IFPs) tend to answer "no" or feel more ambivalent in their responses. IFPs generally feel less responsible for ensuring the emotional comfort of the group's newcomers. This makes perfect sense when we consider that FPs see themselves as managers of their own emotions, so it is only natural that they expect others to do the same. FJs, on the other hand, are more inclined to rely on others for emotional support, so they naturally assume that others desire the same.

As we've seen, Fi and Fe also differ with respect to emotional expressiveness. FPs, in being more emotionally independent, tend to restrain and conceal their emotions. They therefore present as more outwardly measured and less animated in their gestures and expressions. FJ expressions are more direct and feeling-laden, conferring a greater sense of urgency or conviction in what they are saying. At times, it can feel like FJs (especially NFJs) have fallen into a motivational speech in the midst of an ordinary conversation.

Fi-Fe differences can sometimes make communication strained or uncomfortable between Fi and Fe types. IFPs can be wary of Fe judgments and expressions. To IFPs, Fe expressions may seem contrived, predictable, melodramatic, or overly opinionated. IFPs have little patience for what they see as showy or disingenuous emotional displays. This is why they exempt themselves from certain Fe norms or conventions that they see hindering or compromising emotional authenticity. IFPs may also resist FJ attempts to advise them or to cajole them to talk more openly or directly about emotional issues.

FJs may struggle with IFPs' seeming lack of warmth or helpfulness. For instance, an FJ friend of mine has complained on numerous occasions about IFP sales associates, seeing them as unwelcoming, uncommunicative, and unwilling to go out their way to be helpful.

FJs may also take issue with IFPs' reluctance or inability to be more forthright with their judgments and feelings. They may find themselves wishing that IFPs would simply say what they want or express what they are feeling rather than relying on hints or other indirect clues. More specifically, they may bemoan IFPs' propensity for moodiness and causing others to "walk on eggshells," while being unwilling to directly express their feelings or address the problem at hand. Such displays of passive-aggressiveness are foreign and bemusing to the more direct and forthright FJ types.

Fe & the Brain

According to Dario Nardi, FJs' brain activity reflects a concern for interpersonal matters and social responsibilities. More specifically, Nardi's research reveals the following characteristics of FJ types:

- Focused on people-related issues and objectives
- Stimulated by communicating explanations and decisions
- Use value-laden language
- Skillfully adjust to social feedback

Nardi also reports that EFJs show activity in one or two brain regions associated with Ti, supporting the theory that Ti and Fe occur and work together as a function pair.

Part IV

ADDITIONAL CLARIFICATION

Chapter 16

TYPE STRUCTURING: WHAT IT TELLS US ABOUT EPS, EJS, IPS, & IJS

A couple years ago, my colleague Elaine Schallock developed the theory that, in the natural order of things, each personality type would move in a more or less sequential fashion through the functions in its functional stack over the course of a day. More specifically, each type would prefer to start the day engaging its dominant function, before eventually moving into its auxiliary, tertiary, and inferior.

Schallock's theory seems to hold true in my personal experience. My preference as an INTP is to work on my writing in the morning and, time permitting, well into the afternoon. Then once my mind fatigues or interest wanes, I naturally turn to S things like household chores, jogging, or yoga. By the time evening rolls around, I'm often ready to engage with other people in conversation (Fe). I've noticed the reverse trend in sensing types, who commonly enjoy exercising and completing physical tasks earlier in the day.

The point is we naturally gravitate toward our type's strengths and preferences early in the day, when we are most refreshed and energized. Moreover, on days when we fail to exercise our core strengths, we often feel dissatisfied, sensing that something essential was left out.

If we apply this line of thinking to the functional stacks of EJs and IPs, these types would start their day in judging mode (Te, Fe, Ti, or Fi), eventually move into auxiliary and tertiary perceiving, and then finish in judging (inferior). EPs and IJs would display the opposite sequence, starting in perceiving (Se, Ne, Si, or Ni), eventually moving into judging, and then returning to perceiving. This prompted Schallock to classify EJs and IPs as "J-P-J" types and EPs and IJs as "P-J-P" types.

In the first part of this chapter, we will explore some of the details and implications of Schallock's theory, including the ramifications of EJs and IPs using a dominant judging function and EPs and IJs wielding a dominant perceiving function. In the second half of the chapter, I will provide general descriptions of EP, EJ, IP, and IJ types, which are intended to integrate some of the J-P nuances and complexities discussed throughout this book.

"J-P-J" Types: EJs & IPs

Dominant Function: J function

Auxiliary & Tertiary: P functions

Inferior Function: J function

As indicated above, EJs and IPs exhibit similarities in the structuring of their functional stacks. They start out with a judging function, move into perceiving, and eventually return to judging (J-P-J).

Considering that their dominant function is a judging function, IPs, like EJs, are in some respects well understood as predominant judgers. IPs are inner judgers, cultivating inner control and order by way of Ti or Fi, while EJs are outer judgers, working to procure outer control through Te or Fe. Just as EJs are sometimes viewed as outer control freaks, IPs are inner control freaks.

While thinking of IPs as predominant judgers may seem confusing or even contradictory, it is less so if you remember that the J-P preference primarily references a type's outer presentation. So even though IPs are judgers inwardly, they remain perceivers outwardly.

As predominant judgers, EJs and IPs work to hammer down what they believe, building a worldview that can inform their purpose and direction. When their worldview or sense of direction is unsettled, they may feel anxious or aimless. This anxiety prompts them to seek J answers, working to restore a comfortable level of closure.

Their dominant judging function also prompts EJs and IPs to take life rather seriously and approach it with intentionality. They are prone to consider various perceiving activities as "wasting time" (e.g., watching television) and certain IJ or EP individuals as lazy or unproductive. At the same time, they may envy IJs' and EPs' ability to relax---to sit back and take life in (i.e., to perceive). Often thinking in terms of what they should be doing, EJs and IPs may struggle with activities they see as lacking a serious purpose (e.g., playing games), especially if asked to do so for extended periods of time. Although they may enjoy perceiving for a while, it's usually not long before they feel compelled to be "productive."

In short, EJs and IPs have difficulty "perceiving for the sake of perceiving." They are more likely to engage in what we might call "perceiving with a purpose." An IP author, for instance, might read certain books or research articles that she sees as necessary for informing or advancing her work. EJs and IPs are less likely to read (or partake in other perceiving activities) for the simple pleasure of doing so. Instead, their perceiving activities are often framed as contributing to their personal enrichment or as furthering their current or future objectives. Even playing with their children may be framed in J terms such as "bonding time." Hence, J-P-J types tend to use perceiving as a means to a felt or imagined J end.

It is rarely long after waking that EJs' and IPs' dominant J function works to identify what its first objective will be. Thus, when it comes to initiating tasks, IPs can be as disciplined and intentional as EJs. It is mainly after starting a task that IPs get sidetracked and start looking more like EPs. This is understandable in light of the fact that their auxiliary function is more divergent and open-ended in nature (Ne or Se). Their tendency to get sidetracked or lack follow-through can be a source of frustration for IPs, since the endpoint of their functional stack (e.g., their inferior Te or Fe function) represents a state of closure. This desired state of closure might entail finishing a project, making a firm decision, or finding a "once and for all" answer. This is why I suggested in Chapter 6 that IPs "seek, but struggle to obtain, closure."

Their inferior function's push for closure can make EJs and IPs prone to impatience and to rushing through their work. IPs, in particular, may feel that if they don't work quickly they may lose motivation and fail to finish. Quick work and short-cuts also bespeak the J tendency to "get to the point" or "cut to the chase." Unfortunately, a sense of J urgency can contribute to myriad errors and oversights, as well as poorer quality work.

Visually, the J-P-J process resembles a diamond. It starts with a specific objective (J), diverges outwardly (P), and then converges back toward a point of closure (J). We can summarize this in the following way:

Start with Dominant J Function: Intentionality, e.g., "I should or want to do..."

Move into Auxiliary / Tertiary P Tunctions: May get sidetracked (especially IPs)

Endpoint (Inferior J): Desired point of closure

"P-J-P" Types: EPs & IJs

Dominant Function: P function

Auxiliary & Tertiary: J functions

Inferior Function: P function

EPs and IJs also exhibit similarities in the structuring of their functional stacks. They start out with a perceiving function, move into judging, and eventually return to perceiving (P-J-P). In light of the fact that their dominant function is a perceiving function, IJs, like EPs, are in some respects well understood as predominant perceivers. More specifically, IJs are "inner perceivers."

As predominant perceivers, IJs, like EPs, can struggle when it comes to initiating tasks or projects. Just as it is difficult for IPs and EJs to "perceive for the sake of perceiving," it can be difficult for IJs and EPs to "judge for the sake of judging." While J-P-J types may see perceiving as somewhat "unproductive," IJs and EPs tend to see things differently. For them, perceiving is both productive and enjoyable in its own right. It is productive in the sense that *effective action or sound judgments demand accurate perception.* And because accurate perception often takes time, including the collection and consideration of ample information, they see no need to rush into judgments.

While IJs and EPs undoubtedly love to perceive, there are times when they would like to create or accomplish something but lack the necessary motivation or stimulation to move into judging. They may have good ideas or intentions, but never get around to expressing or enacting them. Indeed, there may be times when they envy IPs' and EJs' ability to readily develop and dive into J projects. Granted, not all IJs and EPs will struggle with jumpstarting their own projects, especially those with a strong thirst for achievement or ego gratification (e.g., Steve Jobs). But in many cases, they seem to need a stronger push, be it from within or without, to get the ball rolling in the direction of what we might call "J productivity."

EPs and IJs are less concerned with actively seeking closure than EJs and IPs. This is due to the fact that both their dominant and inferior functions are perceiving functions. So not only do they prefer perceiving on the front end by way of the dominant function, but their desired endpoint (i.e., the inferior) is also a state of perceiving.

A signature strength of the P-J-P process is patience. Since IJs and EPs don't experience the same urge for closure that J-P-J types do, they tend to be more patient in their work, prioritizing accuracy over speed and quality over quantity. Their focus on quality and accuracy may translate into perfectionism or meticulousness. This is especially common among IJs, but is also evident in some EPs.

Visually, the P-J-P process resembles an *hourglass*. It begins with a state of relaxed perceiving (P), transitions into a state of judging or more focused behavior (J), and then reverts back to a state of perception (P):

> <u>Start with Dominant P Function</u>: A state of relaxed perceiving
>
> <u>Move into Auxiliary / Tertiary J functions</u>: Judging / focused behavior
>
> <u>Endpoint (Inferior P)</u>: Desired state of perception

EP Types

In light of the above discussion, EPs are well conceived as the "purest" perceivers of all the types. Not only do they display perceiving in their outer behavior and demeanor (e.g., open, adaptable, receptive, etc.), but their dominant function (Ne or Se) is also a perceiving function.

As dominant perceivers, EPs tend to be less proactive (in the J sense) than EJs or IPs. Rather than formulating goals or initiating action on the front end, their natural propensity is to wait for something to spur them into action. Consider, for example, the ESP firefighter, who routinely awaits new emergencies, or the ENP journalist who patiently waits for a good story to come her way. As extraverted perceivers, many EPs find that walking, driving, or being around people helps kick-start their perceptive juices. Others may turn to various forms of media and entertainment for stimulation.

ESPs are wired to adapt and respond to immediate circumstances, to "fly by the seat of their pants." This often involves some form of physical action, which is why they make great athletes, performers, and emergency responders. ENPs, by contrast, are geared to respond in more abstract ways, such as proffering new ideas, options, or possibilities. While it is most natural and optimal for ESPs to respond in S ways and ENPs in N ways, the inferior function may occasionally incite these types to go against the grain of their dominant function.

The inferior function may cause ENPs to feel torn between the familiar (Si) and novel (Ne), the past (Si) and the future (Ne), the conventional (Si) and the unconventional (Ne). To a certain extent, ENPs get attached to the traditions and patterns of their childhood (Si), even if largely subconsciously. At the same time, their Ne prompts them to question everything and explore alternatives. This can contribute to significant identity confusion among ENPs, who may struggle to discern how far they should break from their past (Si) versus open-endedly exploring alternative ideas and possibilities (Ne).

Similarly, ESPs must strike a balance between their dominant Se and inferior Ni. They can be seen as working to reconcile divergent outer perception (Se) with convergent inner perception (Ni). Their Se seeks to experience the material world in all its forms and diversity, whereas Ni is concerned with extracting deep and abstract meanings and explanations. Se focuses on the way things appear on the surface, while Ni peers beneath appearances to apprehend something deeper. ESPs may therefore feel torn between broadly exploring sensory novelties (Se) and developing a deeper sense of knowing and understanding (Ni). At times, their inferior Ni may, for better or worse, inspire them to seek work as advisors, counselors, ministers, etc., vocations associated with wisdom and insight.

EJ Types

If EPs are the purest perceivers, EJs are the purest judgers. Not only do EJs display judging in their outer behavior and demeanor (e.g., firm, opinionated, directive, etc.), but their dominant function (Te or Fe) is also a judging function, which contributes a proactive, intentional approach to life. For EJs and EPs alike, "what you see is what you get," that is, their outer personality is typically an accurate reflection of who they really are.

EJs are born leaders and teachers. They are direct, uninhibited, and outwardly confident. At times, others may see them as pushy or overbearing. They are also highly intentional and goal-oriented, which can beget impatience and frustration when things diverge from their expected agenda. In the presence of EJs, others may feel rushed or hurried, sensing that the EJ wants them to "cut to the chase."

Despite their outer confidence and imposing presence, EJs are no more inwardly secure or sure of themselves than other types. In fact, because their inner judging function (Ti or Fi) is inferior, they may be deeply insecure. Finding inner control elusive, they naturally turn their focus outwardly, hoping that achieving outer control will somehow translate into inner peace and security. Of course, controlling the outer world is not always easy, which keeps some EJs in a perpetual state of hypervigilance.

As we saw with the EP types, EJs must constantly reckon with the needs and desires of their inferior function. When indulging their inferior Fi or Ti, EJs can get mired in a state of trying to help, fix, or control themselves. When this occurs, their focus shifts from one of outer control, which comes rather naturally to them, to one of grasping for inner control or self-sufficiency.

EFJs' chief psychological struggle consists of forging a balance between their dominant Fe and inferior Ti, between interdependence (Fe) and independence (Ti), managing others (Fe) and managing themselves (Ti). In the grip of Ti, the usually social EFJ can suddenly become aloof and self-consumed. They may bury themselves in stacks of books in hopes of honing their logic or augmenting their sense of self-control. At times, this may even cause them to mistype as introverts or thinkers.

For ETJs, the struggle is one of managing external systems and operations (Te) versus exploring and handling their personal feelings (Fi). In the grip of Fi, the typically outer-directed ETJ may become mired in his or her emotions. Such feelings often have a negative tone and may manifest as bouts of sulking, self-pity, moodiness, or low self-esteem. Occasionally, their inferior Fi may cause ETJs to misidentify as introverts or feelers.

IP Types

As we've seen, IPs are a mixture of J-P characteristics. While their auxiliary Se or Ne begets an outwardly receptive attitude, their dominant Ti or Fi contributes to their status as "inner judgers." And because their judgments are introverted in direction, they typically remain concealed from others, leaving others with little clue as to what they are thinking or feeling. In contrast to EJs and EPs, what you see is not really what you get with IPs (or IJs for that matter). For introverts, their extraverted presentation belies their true inner nature.

Because their extraverted judging function (Fe or Te) is inferior, IPs are the slowest of all types to express their judgments. This is why IPs are commonly viewed as patient and receptive listeners. Their outer passivity and receptiveness can make them easy targets for extraverts or J types looking for a listening ear. But IPs are not always as eager to listen as their appearance might suggest. As inner Js, they are not nearly as passive or relaxed inwardly as they may appear outwardly. Their inner J contributes an inner seriousness and sense of intentionality. Indeed, this is a common reason IPs mistype as IJs; they mistake their inner judging process (i.e., self-directed Fi or Ti) for IJs' external judging process (i.e., outer-directed Fe or Te).

In many respects, IPs are "inner control freaks." They are the most independent of all types with respect to their logical (ITPs) or feeling-based judgments (IFPs). Thus, when others make demands of them, they can become frustrated or even resentful. Such demands disrupt their self-directed judging process and force them to shift their attention outwardly. IPs deplore being forced to face externalities that they would rather avoid or approach on their own terms. In such instances, they may think to themselves: "I wish people would just leave me alone and let me do things my own way."

IPs' penchant for control can at times be irksome to others, especially in situations involving group planning. Since IPs are not terribly keen on planning and dislike making decisions that affect others, they can be less than enthusiastic when it comes to doing their fair share of planning for a group event. Then, after plans have already been forged, it is not uncommon for IPs to hint or complain about how they would have done things differently. Hence, when it comes to doing things with others, IPs are conflicted. On the one hand, they want to be in control in order to avoid being controlled by others' decisions. On the other hand, they abnegate control because they don't like making decisions or being responsible for others.

These same control issues tend to surface in IPs' work lives. Namely, since they don't like being controlled or criticized by others, it can be difficult for them to function as employees (especially ITPs). In response, they may try their hand at management in order to avoid being controlled; they exchange being the controlee for being the controller. The problem with this is IPs are not authentically interested in managing others. While it may give their inferior function (Te or Fe) a temporary ego boost, management is not an authentic IP activity; self-management is, managing others is not. It is generally better to allow extraverts or J types to take care of the managing, freeing IPs to seek or create work that allows them to function more autonomously.

Like other types, IPs partake in an ongoing drama between their dominant and inferior functions. While understanding their control issues, as just described, is a good first step toward personal growth, IPs can also benefit from understanding their type's dominant-inferior dynamics.

For IFPs, the Fi-Te function pair creates a tension between personal judgments (Fi) on the one hand, and collective methods and standards (Te) on the other. IFPs typically emphasize the former, championing the unique tastes and preferences of the individual (Fi), but they can also be enticed by standardized methods and operations (Te). IFPs also experience a tension between their personal needs and interests (Fi) and their sense of collective duty and responsibility (Te). Those over-identifying with their inferior Te may highlight the degree to which they are dutiful, responsible, smart (read logical), or organized. At times, this may lead them to mistype as IFJs, ITPs or, less commonly, as ITJs.

The challenge for ITPs is reconciling Ti and Fe. This involves a balancing act between self (Ti) and others (Fe), independence (Ti) and relationships (Fe), self-mastery (Ti) and external acclaim (Fe). While ITPs undoubtedly need other people, they may fail to consistently acknowledge this need or invest in their relationships. This can result in a pattern of broken or abandoned relationships, or, at its worst, complete social isolation. Furthermore, the inferior function may beckon ITPs to generalize (Fe) their own Ti views or methods, which may include grandiose dreams of fame or recognition (Fe). It can also engender naïve views of love, manifesting as childlike sentimentalism or romantic idealism. ITPs' status as inner judgers may at times lead them to mistype as J types, while their inferior Fe may contribute to their mistyping as feelers. For an in-depth look at ITP inferior function issues, see my books, *The INTP* and *The INTP Quest*.

IJ Types

IJs are also a mixture of J-P characteristics. Outwardly, they are judgers, well deserving of the J label. They can be firm, direct, and outspoken, at times even resembling EJ types. But since their dominant function is a perceiving function (Ni or Si), they can also be understood as "inner perceivers."

As inner perceivers, IJs' primary goal is not one of control or action, but of perception; they inwardly perceive before they outwardly judge. Just as IPs' inner J is rather serious and intentional, IJs' inner P is more carefree and playful. They are far less closed or serious inwardly than they appear outwardly.

IJs' perceptive nature may be most easily discerned in childhood. An INFJ friend of mine, for instance, recounts spending countless hours alone in her room engrossed in her imagination and playing with percepts through drawing and painting. Similarly, an ISTJ friend spent much of his childhood immersed in perceiving, avidly following an array of college and professional sports teams, including glutting himself on sports-related facts and statistics. He is now a play-by-play commentator for a minor league baseball team.

While IPs start the day with a judging mindset (Ti or Fi), IJs prefer a more leisurely and perceptive approach (Ni or Si), allowing their judging process (Fe or Te) to emerge organically or spontaneously rather than intentionally. Therefore, when it comes to initiating the judging process, IJs may patiently wait (or delay) as long as EPs do.

To illustrate, an INTJ once told me that his ideal day would consistent mostly of open-ended perceiving, with periodic interruptions to help others analyze and troubleshoot problems. The image this brings to mind is one of sage or advisor, an individual who patiently waits for problems to emerge that his Ni and Te can then work to resolve. From this we can see that IJs, as predominant perceivers, IJs are in some respects like EPs. The primary difference is that IJs respond with analysis whereas EPs are wired to respond with action (ESPs) or potential options (ENPs).

Like other types, IJs must navigate a perpetual drama between their dominant and inferior function. INJs work to balance their dominant Ni with their inferior Se, to integrate convergent inner perception (Ni) with divergent outer perception (Se). This is sometimes experienced as a struggle between analyzing and interpreting the world from afar (Ni) and acting in a concrete way (Se). INJs often worry that they aren't really living life, but merely observing it from the sidelines. They feel conflicted about the degree to which they can or should act (Se) in order to actualize or materialize their Ni ideals.

Like ENPs, ISJs strive to reconcile the "tried and true" (Si) with the new and novel (Ne). In the following Personality Junkie excerpt, Elaine Schallock describes ISJs' relationship with their inferior Ne: "ISJs are usually not apt to engage in truly radical or risky thoughts or behavior. Their explorations into the realm of Ne are generally limited to ideas that don't risk challenging their beliefs or core principles. Getting an ISJ to try something new can be a crapshoot; depending on the perceived riskiness of the activity and the openness of their inferior Ne to take on the unknown, an ISJ may or may not be open to trying or learning something new. More often, ISJs latch onto a favorite belief or pastime and proceed to work endless variations (Ne) of the same basic theme. Friends and family may thus all end up with the same home-made teapot cozy but each in a different color or pattern."

Summary

What follows is a summary of some distinguishing characteristics of EPs, EJs, IPs, and IJs that may prove useful in discerning your type:

EPs:

- Utilize P-J-P process
- "Purest" perceivers
- Prefer a state of outer perception or perception combined with physical action (ESPs)
- Outwardly open, adaptable, and informal
- Neither strongly seek nor readily experience convergence in beliefs / worldview (especially ENPs)
- Least concerned of all types with external order / structure (especially ENPs)

EJs:

- Utilize J-P-J process
- "Purest" judgers
- Take a pro-active, intentional approach to the outside world
- Outwardly direct, firm, assertive, and opinionated
- Seek, experience, and exhibit convergence in beliefs / worldview
- Seek and prefer external structure, the nature of which may vary by T-F preference

IPs:

- Utilize J-P-J process
- Mixture of J and P characteristics
- Take a pro-active, intentional approach toward their interests and ordering their inner world

- Outwardly receptive, adaptable, and informal
- Seek, but struggle to obtain (especially INPs), convergence in beliefs / worldview
- May appreciate some degree of external structure, but mostly when self-initiated

IJs:

- Utilize P-J-P process
- Mixture of J and P characteristics
- Prefer a state of relaxed, inner perception
- Outwardly direct, firm, and opinionated
- Do not strongly seek, but experience and exhibit, convergence in beliefs / worldview
- Prefer / tolerate external structure, but inconsistent in actively procuring it

Appendix I

TYPE CLARIFIER ASSESSMENT

The purpose of this assessment is to help you identify your four-letter personality type. It is unique in that it assesses your preferences (Part I) and your functions (Part II), then shows you how to cross-check your results. Remember, it is important to confirm and clarify your type through other means described in this book.

Part I. Preference Clarifier

For the following 36 items, select the letter associated with the word or phrase that best describes your historical personality. Try not to overthink your responses. If you are unsure of how to respond, you can leave the item unmarked.

1.

   c. Compete

   d. Cooperate

2.

   e. Details

   f. Overview

3.

   a. Teach

   b. Facilitate

4.

   g. Self

   h. Group

5.

   d. Helping

   c. Advancing

6.

   e. Actual

   f. Potential

7.

   a. Plan ahead

   b. Improvise

8.

   d. Sympathize

   c. Strategize

9.

   f. Envision

   e. Enact

10.

   g. One great friend

   h. Many good friends

11.

    a. Direct

    b. Indirect

12.

    f. Theory

    e. Practice

13.

    c. Achievement

    d. Compassion

14.

    g. Inner world

    h. Outer world

15.

    e. Tangible

    f. Abstract

16.

    d. Beautiful

    c. Useful

17.

    g. Anxious in the world

    h. At home in the world

18.

    f. Idea

    e. Reality

19.

    h. Work with others

    g. Work independently

20.

    c. Utility

    d. Morality

21.

    g. Self-conscious

    h. Unhesitating

22.

    d. Emotional

    c. Logical

23.

    g. Alone time

    h. "Out and about"

24.

    e. Doing

    f. Imagining

25.

    c. Optimize

    d. Empathize

26.

    e. Facts

    f. Theory

27.

a. Standardized

b. Makeshift

28.

e. Down-to-earth

f. Absent-minded

29. When surrounded by noise or commotion I tend to feel…

h. Calm, composed, and comfortable

g. Anxious, overwhelmed, or unsettled

30. At work or school, others see me as more…

b. Open, receptive, and casual

a. Orderly, direct, and serious

31. In social situations, I tend to stay in the…

g. Background

h. Foreground

32. After making a decision or drawing a conclusion, I…

a. Typically don't change my mind, at least not in a major way

b. Often end up questioning, even overturning, my original judgment

33. In emotional situations I tend to…

d. Feel others' emotions

c. Feel uncomfortable or inadequate

34. In social situations I tend to…

b. Adapt to and blend with other people

a. Assert my own views or wishes

35. In general…

c. I prefer not to be bothered with others' personal needs

d. I feel responsible for or compelled to meet others' needs

36. When asked to plan for a group vacation I would likely…

a. Plan carefully and thoroughly, perhaps even formulating a timeline or agenda

b. Plan only a rough outline, expecting to figure out everything else "on the fly"

Scoring

Total your responses for each letter below:

a_____

b_____

c_____

d_____

e_____

f_____

g_____

h_____

Interpretation

If g > h, your preference is likely introversion (I).

If h > g, your preference is likely extraversion (E).

If e > f, your preference is likely sensing (S).

If f > e, your preference is likely intuition (N).

If c > d, your preference is likely thinking (T).

If d > c, your preference is likely feeling (F).

If a > b, your preference is likely judging (J).

If b > a, your preference is likely perceiving (P).

Record your four preferences below:

_____   _____   _____   _____

If you are confident in your results, this may well be your personality type. To confirm or further clarify your type, continue to Part II.

Part II. Function Clarifier

To clarify your preferred functions, rank the following eight descriptions from 1-8, with *1 being the most descriptive* of your historical personality and *8 being the least.*

a.___I am a take-charge, no-nonsense type of person. I'm not afraid to take the lead or issue directives or correctives to others. My mind seems to work quite efficiently and decisively. It is typically easy for me to make decisions, give advice or instructions, and get things done without getting bogged down with emotional concerns. Others see me as firm and forthright, perhaps even blunt. I enjoy staying busy and using my time effectively. On the whole, I take a rational approach to life and can feel uncomfortable or inadequate in emotional situations. I'm more inclined to offer advice than to spend time commiserating. Consequently, I'm most comfortable in work-related situations, especially when analyzing problems, completing tasks, or issuing directives. I also enjoy thinking about strategies and logistics, or ways of making systems or processes more efficient and productive.

b.___ In some respects, I feel like an alien in the world. I am more of an observer and analyzer of life than a participant. This can make it scary for me to act or make big changes in my life. Typically, my mind is fairly zen-like, characterized by a state of relaxed awareness that straddles the conscious and unconscious mind. In this state, my mind is not restless or flooded with random ideas, but is generally calm and synchronized. When presented with a problem, my mind works in a unified way to simultaneously see different perspectives and "realize" answers. At times, these answers or insights can come suddenly and all at once, like a tidal wave of knowing; for me, there is a real difference between *believing* something and *knowing* something. I can get discouraged, however, when others don't seem to understand or respond to my insights with a similar sense of conviction. In many cases, people seem to disregard my insights, suggest I'm being too negative or pessimistic, or think I'm blowing things out of proportion. But I'm simply being honest, calling things as I see them, and in most cases, I'm eventually proven right. Indeed, I see it as my primary role to perceive things accurately and correct false perceptions—to bring the truth to light. Despite seeming opinionated and strong-minded, it is not unusual for others to turn to me for answers, insights, or advice.

c.___I spend a fair amount of time surveying and weighing my personal feelings and values. Since it is important that I live a moral and authentic life, I see it as important to consider exactly what that means and might look like for me. I need time to listen to what my heart and conscience tell me is right. I think the world would be a better place if everyone learned to tune into his or her inner moral compass. Part of my moral code involves "fighting for the underdogs"—those who are poor, sick, disabled, victims of injustice, or otherwise find themselves in unfortunate circumstances. I also enjoy caring for children, plants, animals, or whatever personally affects or moves me. I have the ability to deeply empathize with others. When I imagine myself in others' shoes, I feel for them and it inspires me to respond. Others typically see me as a good listener—empathetic and non-judgmental. At times, I can feel emotionally over-burdened, having internalized others' pain and struggles. When it comes to emotions, I tend to be more of a receiver than an a expresser. I manage my feelings on my own rather than unloading them onto others. I therefore feel that most people don't really know me or see what is most important to me.

d.___I am a "people person." I'm generally warm and personable, with a knack for making quick connections with people. I like to talk and routinely enjoy conversation with friends, family, co-workers, and even strangers. Generally speaking, I am firm and forthright in expressing my views and opinions. While typically tactful, I am reluctant to let my voice go unheard. I enjoy teaching, managing, and directing people, helping them to be and achieve their very best. In many ways, I feel responsible for the emotional well-being and success of others. I want them to excel, both individually and interpersonally. I enjoy finding ways of bringing people together, helping them communicate and get on the same emotional page. If I'm being honest, I'm really not as good at listening to others as I am at advising or teaching them. On more than one occasion, I have been guilty of giving unsolicited advice or opening my mouth when I probably shouldn't have. Nevertheless, people often turn to me for support and guidance regarding their lives and relationships.

e.___I am generally a person of routine. I see no problem with continuing to do things the way they have been done in the past, with sticking to the "tried and true." Doing so makes life simpler and keeps things consistent. I tend to agree with the old saying, "If it ain't broke don't fix it!" I don't understand why so many people think it's a good idea to modify or abandon time-tested methods or traditions (i.e., The Constitution, religious traditions, etc.). I personally believe that if something has been resilient enough to stand the test of time, it's probably worth preserving and protecting. I enjoy reflecting on my personal past, as well as various traditions—familial, religious, historical, political, etc.—that are important to me. I feel safe, secure, nostalgic, and reassured when I reflect on these things. When it comes to money and material goods, I tend to be fairly conservative. I am typically careful not to be wasteful or extravagant in my expenditures. When it comes to work, I like to know exactly what the rules and procedures are so I can do my job properly. I feel the details of a job are important and should not be ignored or overlooked. Others see me as a loyal, reliable, dutiful, and responsible.

f.___I am a fun-loving person who relishes spontaneous action. I don't waste time over-thinking things. I usually perform better and enjoy myself more when I just do what comes naturally. I love taking in new experiences and sensations—new sights, sounds, tastes, and so on. I enjoy using my hands and losing myself in activities such as sports, sex, cooking, driving, dancing, shopping, exercising, and the like. If given a choice, I prefer to be up and moving around rather than sitting. I tend to get restless fairly quickly and am happier when I'm being active. I'm not a terribly abstract person and have never been a huge fan of book learning. I'd rather learn from experience than from books or lectures. In my view, experience is probably life's best teacher. I'm also a highly observant person. I tend to notice and recall details that others may overlook. Keeping pace with current styles and fashions is also fun for me, including things like trendy cars, phones, fashions, hairstyles, decor, etc.

g.___Independence, autonomy, and personal freedom are among my highest values; some people might even call me a loner. While I have little interest or aptitude in leading or managing others, I also don't want people controlling me or telling me what to do. When working within a system or organization, I often find myself at odds with it and end up looking for ways to circumvent what I see as unnecessary rules or inefficient methods. This of course can be anxiety-producing, so working for myself is probably my best option. Perhaps more than anything, I want to find work that I enjoy; my work is of utmost importance to me. Unfortunately, finding my ideal work has been difficult due to my strong need for autonomy, as well recurrent indecisiveness about what I should be doing. Efficiency is another of my top priorities. Thinking of time as a currency for accomplishment, I can be rather impatient when it comes to navigating unexpected hurdles or obstacles. Outwardly, I present as easygoing and affable, readily adapting and meshing to the social context. Inwardly, I am far more serious and resolute, constantly thinking about my work or projects and what my next step should be.

h.___I have a restless and active (some might even say hyperactive) mind. It is constantly generating new ideas and seeing new connections, associations, and possibilities ("the possibilities are endless!"). I often see random connections or parallels between things that others fail to see or appreciate. I love playing with words, ideas, associations, and quips. Compelled to explore and exhaust all the options and possibilities, I struggle to make decisions or draw firm conclusions. When a promising new idea or possibility comes to me, I tend to get really excited and want to share it with others. Unfortunately, the excitement often wanes once the novelty wears off or the idea proves less tenable. These ups and downs can make it hard for me to stick with one thing or to finish what I start. Since I tend to bounce from one idea and interest to the next, I sometimes wonder if I'll ever accomplish anything important. I know I have a lot of creative potential, but I often struggle to harness and focus it. Others may see me as quirky, chatty, distractible, inquisitive, creative, unconventional, and open-minded.

Scoring

Record your rankings below:

____ a. = Te

____ b. = Ni

____ c. = Fi

____ d. = Fe

____ e. = Si

____ f. = Se

____ g. = Ti

____ h. = Ne

Integrating Part I & Part II

Before proceeding further, you may wish to consult Appendix II to identify the dominant and auxiliary functions of your personality type from Part I. After doing so, follow these instructions:

1. Compare your top-ranked function with the dominant function of your type from Part I. If they match, you have likely confirmed your type.

2. If your top-ranked function matches the auxiliary function of your type from Part I, or if your second-ranked function matches the dominant function of your type from Part I, you may need to further clarify your E-I or other preferences.

3. If neither your top nor second-ranked function matches the dominant or auxiliary function of your type from Part I, you may need to further clarify your J-P or other preferences.

Additional Considerations

In most cases, results from Part II do not perfectly align with each of the functions in your type's functional stack. This does not mean that type theory is wrong, but only that, for reasons we discussed in Chapter 1, personality testing is not an exact science.

One reason Part I and Part II results may fail to match is the confounding influence of one's E-I preference. For instance, an INTJ might rightly rank Ni first, but select Ti (rather than the predicted Te) as his second preferred function. This may result from not identifying with various extraverted elements of the Te description (e.g., being a "take-charge" person) and/or identifying with introverted elements of the Ti description (e.g., needing independence and autonomy).

With that said, even when a selected function diverges from what is predicted with respect to its E-I direction, the overall ordering of the *basic* functions (S, N, T, F) often follows that of the functional stack. So even if an INTJ ranks Ti as his second preferred function, this still aligns with the predicted order of his having an N dominant and T auxiliary function.

Here are the actual test results of the INTJ I've been referencing:

1. Ni
2. Ti
3. Fi
4. Ne
5. Te
6. Fe
7. Se
8. Si

For the sake of illustration, I want to make just a couple more observations about these results. First, it is not surprising that, as an introvert, three of his top rankings were introverted functions. Second, it is worth noting how the basic ordering of his functions is generally consistent with the predictions of type theory for an INTJ (i.e., N-T-F-S). This speaks to the value of looking for general trends when working to discern one's type. The last thing I'll mention is that, upon further study and self-exploration, people typically come to see their preferred functions more clearly. Thus, our INTJ might eventually conclude that he does prefer Te over Ti. This reinforces the importance of using a multi-pronged approach to clarifying your type rather than relying solely on personality assessments.

Appendix II

FUNCTIONAL STACKS OF THE 16 TYPES

If you study the functional stacks for a few different personality types, you can familiarize yourself with patterns and logic of how they are organized. Once you understand the rules and patterns, you won't need to memorize each type's functional stack, but will be able to deduce it.

For your convenience, I've included the J-P criteria from the Introduction to help you understand the logic behind the functional stack. This is followed by a list of the functional stacks for all 16 personality types.

1. A given type's J-P designation (i.e., the fourth letter of the type) refers largely to its outer (i.e., extraverted) presentation. Hence, J types will extravert a judging attitude (firm, decisive, opinionated, etc.), while P types will display a perceiving attitude (open, flexible, receptive, etc.).

2. For extraverts, the nature of the dominant function (i.e., its status as a judging or perceiving function) matches their J-P designation. For example, ENTPs' dominant

function, Ne, is a perceiving function and ENTJs'
dominant function, Te, is a judging function.

3. For introverts, things are more confusing, since the nature
    of their dominant function opposes their J-P designation.
    We saw this with INTPs above. Namely, despite being
    classified as a P type, INTPs' dominant function (Ti) is
    a judging function. To understand why INTPs and other
    IPs are considered P rather than J types, see number one
    above.

INFJ

Dominant: Introverted Intuition (Ni)

Auxiliary: Extraverted Feeling (Fe)

Tertiary: Introverted Thinking (Ti)

Inferior: Extraverted Sensing (Se)

INTJ

Dominant: Introverted Intuition (Ni)

Auxiliary: Extraverted Thinking (Te)

Tertiary: Introverted Feeling (Fi)

Inferior: Extraverted Sensing (Se)

INTP

Dominant: Introverted Thinking (Ti)

Auxiliary: Extraverted Intuition (Ne)

Tertiary: Introverted Sensing (Si)

Inferior: Extraverted Feeling (Fe)

ISTP

Dominant: Introverted Thinking (Ti)

Auxiliary: Extraverted Sensing (Se)

Tertiary: Introverted Intuition (Ni)

Inferior: Extraverted Feeling (Fe)

INFP

Dominant: Introverted Feeling (Fi)

Auxiliary: Extraverted Intuition (Ne)

Tertiary: Introverted Sensing (Si)

Inferior: Extraverted Thinking (Te)

ISFP

Dominant: Introverted Feeling (Fi)

Auxiliary: Extraverted Sensing (Se)

Tertiary: Introverted Intuition (Ni)

Inferior: Extraverted Thinking (Te)

ISFJ

Dominant: Introverted Sensing (Si)

Auxiliary: Extraverted Feeling (Fe)

Tertiary: Introverted Thinking (Ti)

Inferior: Extraverted Intuition (Ne)

ISTJ

Dominant: Introverted Sensing (Si)

Auxiliary: Extraverted Thinking (Te)

Tertiary: Introverted Feeling (Fi)

Inferior: Extraverted Intuition (Ne)

ENFP

Dominant: Extraverted Intuition (Ne)

Auxiliary: Introverted Feeling (Fi)

Tertiary: Extraverted Thinking (Te)

Inferior: Introverted Sensing (Si)

ENTP

Dominant: Extraverted Intuition (Ne)

Auxiliary: Introverted Thinking (Ti)

Tertiary: Extraverted Feeling (Fe)

Inferior: Introverted Sensing (Si)

ENFJ

Dominant: Extraverted Feeling (Fe)

Auxiliary: Introverted Intuition (Ni)

Tertiary: Extraverted Sensing (Se)

Inferior: Introverted Thinking (Ti)

ESFJ

Dominant: Extraverted Feeling (Fe)

Auxiliary: Introverted Sensing (Si)

Tertiary: Extraverted Intuition (Ne)

Inferior: Introverted Thinking (Ti)

ENTJ

Dominant: Extraverted Thinking (Te)

Auxiliary: Introverted Intuition (Ni)

Tertiary: Extraverted Sensing (Se)

Inferior: Introverted Feeling (Fi)

ESTJ

Dominant: Extraverted Thinking (Te)

Auxiliary: Introverted Sensing (Si)

Tertiary: Extraverted Intuition (Ne)

Inferior: Introverted Feeling (Fi)

ESFP

Dominant: Extraverted Sensing (Se)

Auxiliary: Introverted Feeling (Fi)

Tertiary: Extraverted Thinking (Te)

Inferior: Introverted Intuition (Ni)

ESTP

Dominant: Extraverted Sensing (Se)

Auxiliary: Introverted Thinking (Ti)

Tertiary: Extraverted Feeling (Fe)

Inferior: Introverted Intuition (Ni)

REFERENCES & RESOURCES

To learn more about *The 16 Personality Types*, including their careers, relationships, and type development, I encourage you to visit us at PersonalityJunkie.com. There, you can also take additional personality tests and explore our other books.

Aron, Elaine. *The Highly Sensitive Person*. Broadway Books. 1997.

Csikszentmihalyi, Mihaly. *Flow: The Psychology of Optimal Experience.* Harper. 2008.

Drenth, A.J. *The 16 Personality Types: Profiles, Theory, & Type Development*. Inquire Books. 2013.

Drenth, A.J. *The INTP: Personality, Careers, Relationships, & the Quest for Truth and Meaning*. Inquire Books. 2013.

Drenth, A.J. *The INTP Quest: INTPs' Search for their Core Self, Purpose & Philosophy.* Inquire Books. 2016.

Jung, Carl. *Psychological Types.* Princeton University Press. 1971.

Kagan, Robert. *Galen's Prophecy: Temperament in Human Nature.* Westview Press. 1997.

Myers, Isabel Briggs, et al. *The MBTI Manual: A Guide to the Development and Use of the Myers-Briggs Type Indicator.* CPP. 2003.

Nardi, Dario. *Neuroscience of Personality: Brain Savvy Insights for All Types of People.* Radiance House. 2011.

Pirsig, Robert. *Zen and the Art of Motorcycle Maintenance.* Harper Torch. 2006.

Thomson, Lenore. *Personality Type: An Owner's Manual.* Shambhala. 1998.